WORK OF INFLUENCE

PRINCIPLES FOR PROFESSIONALS FROM THE BOOK OF DANIEL

BY
DAVID A. CROSS

PRAISE FOR
WORK OF INFLUENCE

"Having served Christ for over thirty years in the business world with a heart for the unreached, I found *Work of Influence* to be extremely biblical, practical, and profound. The twenty-five principles drawn from the book of Daniel are both instructional and inspirational to anyone who wants to serve Christ and integrate their work and faith in reaching the world's Unreached People Groups. The task is great, but our God is so much greater!"

Bruce McKenzie
Senior Vice President, Wealth Management
Northern Trust Company

"Business people have felt like second-class citizens in the church for a long time. *Work of Influence* helps us understand that God ordained the business role for many of us to internationally bring blessing and the Gospel to those we touch. This may very well be a central strategy for reaching the remaining unreached groups of the world."

Durwood Snead
Businessman and Pastor
North Point Ministries

"Have you thought about your role in the Great Commission and how it might intersect with your life in the marketplace? If so, this book will challenge you to think strategically about how one can fuel the other. Perhaps never before have there been as many open doors as there are now, in our globalized world. David highlights these open doors while laying out a firm biblical picture of God's desire to see tentmakers take the Gospel to the nations."

Ted Esler, Ph.D.
President
Missio Nexus

"*Work of Influence* helps make the book of Daniel come alive and become relevant for those of us in the workplace. We are reminded through these twenty-five principles that work isn't confined to SUPPORT missions; it is missions."

Chi-Chung Keung
Director News Media and
Senior Communications Counsel
California State University, Fullerton
Board Chair, Pioneers USA

"David's call is to see work—whatever it is—as a work of influence. God wants to do great things through work. When we understand a biblical vision of work, we embrace the understanding that whatever we do, we can work heartily for the Lord through this work."

Justin A. Irving, Ph.D.
Director, Doctor of Ministry Program
Professor of Ministry Leadership
Initiative Director, Bethel Work with Purpose

"The message David is highlighting is one that is necessary to follow if we are to change the reality of those who have not, nor will not, hear or see the Gospel lived out. It goes beyond accessibility and credibility to simple obedience to a Biblical mandate with countless examples of how God worked with His people throughout history. I am praying for many more voices like David's to be raised up to engage our generation in their God-ordained purpose on this planet."

Andrew Scott
Author of Scatter: Go Therefore and Take Your Job with You
President/CEO, Operation Mobilization USA

About the Author

David Cross is president of Professionals Global, an organization that mobilizes, equips, and mentors tentmakers. He writes from fifteen years of missions experience, most of which were as a tentmaker in the Middle East and the United States. His passion for Scripture led him to obtain B.A. degrees in Bible and Biblical Studies from the University of Northwestern - Saint Paul as well as an M.A. in Linguistics from the University of North Dakota. Cross is also author of *Mondays in the Middle East: The Lighter Side of Arabian Nights* and contributor to *The Desert is Alive: Streams of Living Water from Muscat to Marrakech*. His hobbies include hiking and gardening with his wife and five children in Orlando, Florida.

ACKNOWLEDGEMENTS

THERE ARE MANY PEOPLE to whom I am indebted for their influence in making this book possible. At the risk of omitting some who have undoubtedly left an indelible mark on my understanding of work and faith, I would like to specifically thank the following.

The book's formation and structure were greatly enhanced by the early feedback from Durwood Snead. Durwood, you provided great advice on how to make the book most useful to readers. Thank you.

Justin Irving, your friendship has been one of the deepest relationships of my life. In myriad ways you have influenced me through your counsel and prayer, and now, the Lord has brought us to our independent passions for the integration of work and faith. I appreciate not just your thoughtful words included in this book but the brotherhood that underlies your influence in my life.

Thank you, Matt Green, for the generous gift of your time and insights to bring about the final published product. Your contribution to the layout and design has added to your counsel through the publication process that has made this book a better product.

Pastor Rick Fiechter, your early input on the manuscript fueled me with energy to make this book readable and impacting for the everyday person in the pews. Thank you for your encouragement, counsel, and friendship.

Bruce McKenzie, you readily latched on to the vision of this book, giving input, feedback, and excited energy that spurred me on in the ongoing improvement process. Thank you for your friendship and uplifting words about this project and the ongoing work of influence that each of us has.

Thank you, Andrew Scott, not only for taking time out of your busy schedule to contribute here but for your encouraging words as we strive toward that goal of seeing the Great Commission finished. It is a privilege to co-labor with you to that end.

I am most deeply indebted to my wife, Cheryl Cross. Cheryl, you've applied your linguistic, literary, instructional, and grammar expertise to sharpen this book while understanding and allowing me freedom in my own style of writing. Only a true editing professional could do this so adeptly. Nonetheless, whatever errors remain are my own responsibility, to be sure, and are likely a result of my own stubborn adherence to grammar rules from my youth. We've enjoyed many wrestlings over format and style since our early dates sitting in the Camp Lake, Wisconsin, public library reading the Oxford English Dictionary together. I love you and appreciate you more than words can ever say.

My life is marked by my Savior. Everything good that I have become is due to his grace and mercy in my life. Jesus, I want all I do to reflect the goodness and excellence of who you are. I am a child just catching a glimmer of all of that excellence now, but I recognize through that glimmer a greatness above all else. May this book, this work of influence, be a tool in your hand to bring others to deep joy in their work of influence for your glory and for their joy.

David Cross
April 2018

εἰς τὴν δόξαν τοῦ θεοῦ

DEDICATION

Written in memory of Norman and Mildred Buell, my grandparents, whose industrious nature taught me the dignity of hard work and faithfulness.

To my mother, Carol Cross, who faithfully lived out those values of tireless hard work in the face of challenging circumstances. I am forever grateful for your deep sacrifices.

CONTENTS

FOREWORD

WORK MATTERS. It is an important part of our daily lives. Some estimate we spend well over 100,000 hours of our lives working. That represents a majority of the waking hours in our adult lives.

Even though work represents a significant percentage of our lives, we often do not take time to evaluate the nature and purpose of this work—the context within which we invest so much of our time. I, for one, want to know that this 100,000+ hour investment matters. I want it to matter for my life. I want it to matter for my family. And, more importantly, I want it to matter in light of God's work in the world.

In this book, *Work of Influence*, my friend David Cross argues for a model of global Christian engagement that reimagines what our lives can look like when the integration of faith and work is authentic and sincere. Challenging a sacred-secular duality that contrasts work that honors God from work that doesn't, David promotes the power of everyday work. This significant work is carried out not just as a platform for ministry but is seen itself as an authentic part of one's ministry globally.

For David, this model of an integrative understanding of work has ancient roots. Models like Daniel in the Bible provide powerful exemplars for us as we seek to live as whole-life disciples of Jesus Christ in our world today. While work can provide a platform for other good outcomes, the work itself is a good to be celebrated and is part of God's mission in this world through His people.

Our work is not a necessary evil or merely a means to other ends. The work itself has value. When Christians gain a vision of whole-life discipleship that affirms the everyday value of work, this becomes a pathway both for loving our neighbor—next door or around the world—and providing what author David Kim calls a plausibility structure for the Gospel. In other words, work done well points others to a God at work in this world and a Gospel that really does work in people's lives.

Lest we think this is a new message that my friend David is pointing us toward, it is important to recognize that these fresh words have deep roots both historically and theologically. On this, Tim Keller points us back to what it means to be made in the image of God. Keller writes:

> Work of all kinds, whether with the hands or the mind, evidences our dignity as human beings—because it reflects the image of God the Creator in us. . . . Work has dignity because it is something that God does and because we do it in God's place, as his representatives. . . . We were built for work and the dignity it gives us as human beings.[1]

It has been this way since the earliest days of humanity. Before the fall ever entered the human story, God placed Adam in the Garden of Eden with instructions to work and keep it. Since these earliest days, we have been tasked with creative, productive, and restorative work in this world as image bearers of the creative, productive, and restorative God we worship.

So what is your work? Do you work with your hands? Do you work with your mind? Is this work compensated? Is this work unpaid? At its core, work is not about compensation but rather contribution. The way you most significantly contribute to the world and serve others is generally through your work.

David's call is to see this work—whatever it is—as a work of influence. God wants to do great things through work. When we understand a biblical vision of work, we embrace the understanding that whatever we do, we can work heartily for the Lord through this work (Colossians 3.23-24). May God bless you as you take this journey with David exploring the work of influence God has for you in this world.

Justin A. Irving, Ph.D.

SECTION 1

INTRODUCTION

WHAT ADVICE WOULD a teenage Israelite slave from 2,600 years ago have that could benefit a senior executive of a multinational corporation in Tokyo? How does a children's story like "Daniel in the Lion's Den" relate to the modern missions movement? Who are the unreached people of the Middle East today and how are they connected to the ancient civilization of Persia?

Work of Influence is a study of the Old Testament book of Daniel, chapters 1-6, from the perspective of tentmakers. These chapters give a unique perspective on a plethora of today's buzzwords in the Christian world, but specifically, tentmaking. They open a world of meaning that can bring value and purpose to the daily grind you face every day, whether serving the Lord internationally or in your home country.

This term 'tentmaking' is actually a New Testament term, but the rich meaning uncovered by the New Testament examples of tentmakers shows that the term describes examples all through the Old and New Testaments. The Apostle Paul is called a tentmaker because his occupation was to make tents. Seems sensible. He shared this occupation with a few of his companions in ministry, and they worked together to support themselves as they preached the Good News of Jesus. They, too, made tents. Makes sense to call them tentmakers.

In present day, the term is used metaphorically to indicate someone who uses an occupation to support herself while sharing the Gospel through her occupation. In this way, a person who goes to a different people group *with the intention of sharing the Gospel through that occupation* is a tentmaker in the same sense that the Apostle Paul used his occupation to share the Gospel through his work.

There are additional facets of tentmaking and different approaches to theological questions related to tentmaking that are beyond the scope of this book. The point here is not to present an exhaustive resource on all things relating to tentmaking. Rather, this book is intended to teach lessons from Daniel to challenge you to engage with the integration of work and faith and the amazing potential this integration has for reaching the world's unreached people groups.

This is my appeal:

Love your work. Love through work.

David Cross, April 2018

LAYING THE GROUNDWORK

BEFORE WE GET too far ahead of ourselves, let's start out with an explanation of some terms that will be important in our discussion. If you haven't gathered already, the present work has a whole lot to do with sharing the Good News of Jesus. If you're not totally up on all of the lingo that has to do with that Good News, this part is for you.

The Good News

The Good News (the Gospel) is this: All people have broken God's law, committing an infinite offense against the infinite Creator. Nonetheless, God controlled all the events of history to send his Son, Jesus, as the promised King. Jesus lived a perfect, sinless life, so he certainly didn't deserve the punishment for sin, which is death. As the Son of God, his perfect, infinite sacrifice of death on a cross fully compensated for the sins of those who trust in him. Their punishment for sin was placed on Jesus. Since this punishment was paid for, it cannot be paid again by our works or any other means. We who trust in him are free from the punishment of sin. When Jesus rose from the dead after three days, he showed that he was victorious over the punishment of sin and everyone who trusts in him will spend eternity with God.

Missionaries

Is a "missionary" biblical? In the strictest sense, no. The reason is that "missionary" is a Latin-based word and the Bible was written in Hebrew, Aramaic, and Greek. So, no, this Latin word is not in the original manuscripts.

As far as the equivalent of missionary, yes, of course it is biblical. The equivalent New Testament word is the Greek word *apostolos* which is translated as apostle. Now, my advanced theology professor, Dr. William Bevier, would correct me saying that *apostle* is a transliteration, not a translation. In other words, *apostle* is just taking the sound of the Greek word and spelling the sound in English. That being said, then, the translation of *apostolos* is "one who is sent out," just like the translation of the Latin word *missionarius* is "one who is sent out."

But, isn't the word *apostle* reserved for those super-spiritual humans who were eyewitnesses of Jesus? Actually, no.

First, all of these eyewitnesses died about 2,000 years ago, which would mean that all missionary work would have stopped 2,000 years ago if the term only referred to them. Second, others are called apostles throughout the New Testament in the sense that they were 'sent ones' as well. Jesus himself was called "the apostle and high priest whom we confess" in Hebrews 3.1 because he was sent from God the Father as the Savior. Titus and others were included in the group of apostles in 2 Corinthians 8.23; Epaphroditus was called an apostle in Philippians 2.25; and Barnabas was included in the discussion of apostles in 1 Corinthians 9.5-6.

So, yes, the idea of a missionary (though not the Latin word) is biblical and the sending of messengers is thoroughly biblical as many were sent out by Jesus (Matthew 10; Luke 10) or by churches (Acts 13). A missionary is one who is sent out to other peoples, nations, families, and languages by the Church to carry the Good News.

Unreached People Groups

The idea of Unreached People Groups is closely tied to the Great Commission that Jesus gave his followers before he was taken up into heaven:

> Then Jesus came up and said to them, "All authority in heaven and on earth has been given to me. Therefore go and make disciples of all nations, baptizing them in the name of the Father and the Son and the Holy Spirit, teaching them to obey everything I have commanded you. And remember, I am with you always, to the end of the age."
>
> *Matthew 28.18-20*

That phrase "make disciples of all nations" doesn't leave any gaps. It includes all the earth, not a selective group and not limited to the nation of Israel as the people of God. Luke's recounting of the Great Commission is no less comprehensive:

> But you will receive power when the Holy Spirit has come upon you, and you will be my witnesses in Jerusalem, and in all Judea and Samaria, and to the farthest parts of the earth."
>
> *Acts 1.8*

Luke, then, strengthens the description to include every place imaginable. This began with Jerusalem where the disciples of Jesus were, it continued to the intermediate locations of nearby Judea and Samaria, and its reach ended only when every last corner of the earth was included.

So, this Great Commission was comprehensive from the beginning. Now, look at the end result in heaven at the end of time where we read the description of the biggest concert crowd on record . . . ever:

> After these things I looked, and here was an enormous crowd that no one could count, made up of persons from every nation, tribe, people, and language, standing before the throne and before the Lamb dressed in long white robes, and with palm branches in their hands. They were shouting out in a loud voice, "Salvation belongs to our God, to the one seated on the throne, and to the Lamb!"
>
> *Revelation 7.9-10*

People from every *nation, tribe, people,* and *language*—that's a lot of people! So, when Jesus gave his followers (you!) the Great Commission, *those* are the people he had in mind to reach, down to the family.

The Unreached People Groups, then, are those nations, tribes, people groups, and languages that haven't heard this Good News in a way that they can understand. Does that mean that if we broadcast a radio message over the earth that we've reached everyone? They've physically heard it, so does that "count"? Not likely. People do hear radio broadcasts, to be sure, and they begin to follow Jesus. I am thrilled when I hear results of such a valuable ministry, but which language do we use? Which language do we leave out? With 7,097 languages spoken in the world today,[2] we're not going to be able to broadcast to all of them.

If we print tracts or Bible translations, will we reach every people group and language and tribe and nation? Again, not likely. Only 3,909 languages have writing systems.[3] Even though that is a lot of literature, all those people groups don't account for everyone in the world.

More often than not, it takes intentional effort by real, live people to physically go to live among Unreached People Groups to share the Good News personally. As attractive as mass ministry systems are, and they are immensely valuable for the Lost, they aren't going to finish the job for the Unreached. We can't ignore the hard work of going to every single nation, tribe, people group, and language to share the truth of what Jesus has done.

More often than not, it takes intentional effort by real, live people to physically go to live among Unreached People Groups to share the Good News personally.

One more important point about the Unreached is that they shouldn't be confused with those that I just mentioned, the Lost. The Unreached are those who have never heard the Good News, and are restricted by physical barriers, political barriers, or language barriers from hearing the Good News.

The Lost

The Lost are those who do not have these barriers and may have even heard the Gospel before but simply do not believe. The Lost are those in places where there are sizable numbers of believers or churches or books or radio programs or TV programs where they can hear the truth. Their spiritual state is the same as the Unreached, but their opportunity is far different.

The 10/40 Window

Coupled with the idea of Unreached People Groups is the term 10/40 Window. When we look at where in the world Unreached People Groups are concentrated, we see that the vast majority of them are across North Africa, Central Asia, and East Asia. The missionary strategist Luis Bush coined the term "10/40 Window" in 1990 to describe the clustering of Unreached People Groups in nations from the 10th latitude north to the 40th latitude north from West Africa to East Asia.[4]

The 10/40 Window: 97% of all people who have no reasonable access to the Gospel.

There are about 3.16 billion people in Unreached People Groups in the entire world.[5] About 3.06 billion of them live in the 10/40 Window: 97% of all people who have no reasonable access to the Gospel. It's pretty easy to see where the need is to fulfill the Great Commission.

In addition to the staggering number of unreached people, 86% of the world's poorest people live in the 10/40 Window. This is defined as those living on less than $200 per year. That Amazon Prime subscription I just paid for is six months' living expenses for one person.

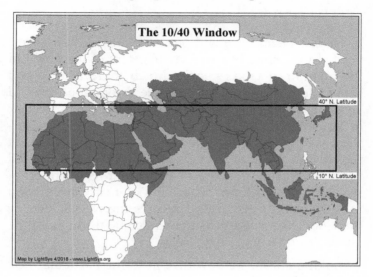

The 10/40 Window

40° N. Latitude

10° N. Latitude

Map by LightSys 4/2018 - www.LightSys.org

How much money goes to send missionaries into this needy part of the world? Andrew Scott, in his book *Scatter,* details some of this for us:

> Americans give 2 percent of their income to Christian causes. . . . Out of that 2 percent, 5 percent goes to ministry outside of the USA; and out of that 5 percent only 1 percent goes toward sharing Jesus with those that have not heard of Him. That is 1% of 5% of 2% = 0.001% of what we earn carefully set aside to ensure those who have never heard the Gospel ever get that critical opportunity.[6]

Statistics like this one are shocking. In order to put them into perspective, we have to develop a new denomination of the American dollar because we don't buy and sell in tenths of pennies. For every hard-earned dollar, we give a mere tenth of one penny to see the lives of the unreached touched by the Gospel.

Summary

These few pages have laid out some of the basic terms needed to discuss our role as followers of Jesus within the mission of God's people. Much more can be said about the mission of God's people throughout the Old Testament and how that relates to the culminating work of Jesus, but these terms are certainly basic prerequisites. We need to know the Gospel before we can share the Gospel. We need to know what missionaries are and their place in sharing the all-important news about Jesus. We need to know what God's Great Commission for us is and how that underscores the task of sharing the Good News with Unreached People throughout the 10/40 Window.

Looking ahead, we now dive in to the particular task of rethinking missions as it relates to our work and our representation of Jesus to the nations.

THE CASE FOR TENTMAKING

Problem to Solve—
Restricted Access Nations

SINCE THE EARLY 1800S and the founding of the modern Christian missions movement, missionaries have admirably been willing to give up everything they have to carry the Good News to the Unreached. This has often entailed very serious hardship through sickness and dangers so that it was common for these missionaries to pack all of their earthly belongings into their own coffin when they left to go overseas. In that case, they were prepared—and even expected—to die among the people they were planning to reach.

In many cases, the governments of these host countries were open to their presence and granted official access through missionary visas. Through the past two hundred years, and especially since the 1960s, this has changed dramatically so that these governments are no longer open to missionaries coming for the sole purpose of sharing their religious beliefs. That being said, these countries expect expatriates from "Christian" countries to be Christians, so it is assumed that they will act as

Christians in their country. It is expected and assumed by these governments that when their people interact with these expatriate workers, they will be hearing about Christianity. For virtually all countries this is not a problem. The problem they have is with people who are sent with the sole purpose of proselytizing, and these governments subsequently restrict access to their countries for these Christians. These "Restricted Access Nations," then, inhibit Christians who are there with no other purpose than to convert the local population. These countries are not restricting access to Christians in general. Believers who are sent to live and work even as Christians are not prevented from living and working in these countries, and this includes interacting on religion.

Since governments have been restricting access to traditional missionaries, a new approach has been adopted across an increasing section of the world: tentmaking, or sharing the Good News through the integration of work and faith. Of course, this isn't a "new" approach at all since it was part of the inception of Christian missions 2,000 years ago. Even so, it has been a long-forgotten approach that is only recently being increasingly used. What's more, it has not always been used as described above, but rather, it has been used mainly as a means of gaining access to a country by getting a visa. In this way, it has been used as a "front" or a platform with an ulterior agenda. Thomas Hale notes in his book *Authentic Lives* that with this hidden identity, "you may feel more like a secret agent than a sent one of Jesus. You may find that your definition of honesty is stretched to the limit."[7] On the other hand, if your motive is to live and work as a follower of Jesus in a foreign country, you don't have an identity to hide. You are using your occupation as a means of living out your best work through your God-given gifts.

Problem to Solve—The Funding Model

Many people look at the prospect of raising personal support and simply run for the hills. To them, tentmaking draws them in because it allows them an opportunity to avoid the uncomfortable prospect of living off of the generosity of others. Even though tentmaking has this as a possible benefit, there are two primary reasons to steer clear of this thinking, namely, the biblical precedent of support and the nature of the calling of God.

First, Jesus lived off of support (Matthew 27.55) and the Apostle Paul lived off of support (e.g. Acts 16.15). It would be hard to appeal to higher authorities or examples.

For Paul, he benefited from the gifts of churches, such as Philippi, for his personal support:

> And as you Philippians know, at the beginning of my gospel ministry, when I left Macedonia, no church shared with me in this matter of giving and receiving except you alone. For even in Thessalonica on more than one occasion you sent something for my need. I do not say this because I am seeking a gift. Rather, I seek the credit that abounds to your account. For I have received everything, and I have plenty. I have all I need because I received from Epaphroditus what you sent—a fragrant offering, an acceptable sacrifice, very pleasing to God. And my God will supply your every need according to his glorious riches in Christ Jesus.
>
> *Philippians 4.15-19*

Paul, then, sets the example of receiving even full support from Church A when planting Church B. He did this with the Philippian church and with the Corinthian church as well (2 Corinthians 11.8).

Some have contended that Paul's words in 1 Corinthians 9 should be normative for all ministry,

> What then is my reward? That when I preach the gospel I may offer the gospel free of charge. . . .
>
> *1 Corinthians 9.18*

However, reading these verses in context shows very clearly that Paul was using these words to *defend* the right of Gospel workers to obtain their living from the Gospel.

> Do we not have the right to financial support? Do we not have the right to the company of a believing wife, like the other apostles and the Lord's brothers and Cephas? Or do only Barnabas and I lack the right not to work? Who ever serves in the army at his own expense? Who plants a vineyard and does not eat its fruit? Who tends a flock and does not consume its milk? Am I saying these things only on the basis of common sense, or does the law not say this as well? For it is written in the law of Moses, "Do not muzzle an ox while it is treading out the grain." God is not concerned here about oxen, is he? Or is he not surely speaking for our benefit? It was written for us, because the one plowing and threshing ought to work in hope of enjoying the harvest.
>
> *1 Corinthians 9.4-10*

They had the same right to support as they had to be married and take along a believing wife. It is clear, then, that some people should make their living from the work of the Gospel.

Second, God is able to provide for his work to be done. If people sense the Lord moving on their hearts to be sent out to share the Good News, finances should not supersede this. The calling of God is a matter of faith. If a person does not have faith that God can provide for the call, it is reasonable to question that faith. In short, tentmaking is not a crutch for those who do not have faith that God will provide.

Accepting, then, that living by support is legitimate for some people, tentmaking is, nonetheless, explosive in its potential for rapidly deploying an army of faithful, effective witnesses to the truth of the Gospel. Most missionaries spend eighteen to twenty-four months or more raising support for living overseas, and many of them wither on the vine, so to speak, and lose the vision, never actually going overseas. Imagine the potential of 5% or 15% or 40% of faithful believers sensing the burden to use their work as their means of outreach to an unbelieving world. Let's not ask for the world, here, though. Imagine 1% of believers sensing this burden. That would still be 100 times as many people as there are working with the unreached today. Using your job without the need for financial support can facilitate this.

Problem to Solve — Authentic Lives

As hinted at earlier in the section on Restricted Access Nations, one of the major challenges to face is going with merely a "platform" that is different than your stated reason for being in a Restricted Access Nation. To many of these governments, this could be perceived as espionage, at worst, but disingenuous and deceitful at least. As an example, I'll share my story with tentmaking.

My bachelor's degrees are in Bible and Biblical Studies. Hearing that, a seasoned tentmaker encouraged me to get a more marketable graduate degree that would provide me access to the Middle East. He emphasized, "Preferably, it would be something where you could spend as little time as necessary in the job so that you could spend more time in ministry." This makes sense on the surface, but there are problems with this approach. First, it devalues the work done in the occupation. Second, it is disingenuous toward the host government since your stated work is not your real work. Third, it sets up a duality in life between sacred and secular, between that work that honors God and that work that doesn't.

A sincere integration between faith and work is traced all the way back to Babylonia in the time of Daniel.

As it happened, I got a graduate degree in linguistics with the intent of teaching linguistics overseas. This would afford the fewest hours in the classroom and minimal effort to keep my lectures up to date. Now, I really do love linguistics, but I have to admit that I probably love it more as a hobby than a career.

That being the case, I would give my younger self different advice. I would say, "If linguistics is something that you feel brings together your unique gifting from the Lord and your contribution to the world, by all means, get a degree in linguistics. If you feel this is the best exercise of who David Cross is, get a degree in linguistics. But if this is just a means to establish a platform to do something else, don't get a degree in linguistics."

This book proposes an approach that diverges from traditional missions and even the "platform tentmaking" popularized since the 1960s. This book teaches a sincere integration between faith and work with a genuineness that is traced all the way back to Babylonia in the time of Daniel.

Tentmaking—In Depth

I mentioned the origin of tentmaking above, but let's look at that a bit closer. In Acts, Paul is referred to as a tentmaker.

> After this Paul departed from Athens and went to Corinth. There he found a Jew named Aquila, a native of Pontus, who had recently come from Italy with his wife Priscilla, because Claudius had ordered all the Jews to depart from Rome. Paul approached them, and because he worked at the same trade, he stayed with them and worked with them *(for they were tentmakers by trade).*
>
> *Acts 18.1-3 (emphasis added)*

Pontus was a region of modern day Turkey that ran along the southern shore of the Black Sea. So, even though the story above picks up in Corinth, Aquila and his wife Priscilla were already a long way from home. Their travels had taken them to Rome where they set up shop, but they were expelled from Rome because of religious persecution. That made Corinth their home away from home away from home. That's life.

Paul found himself coming to Corinth from a different direction, Athens, where they didn't quite roll out the red carpet for him. But he was originally from Tarsus in the region of Cilicia. Cilicia is the Latin name for "hair-cloth"[8] which is what tents were made of, so it makes sense that the trade Paul was taught was the trade of his home region.

As is often the case with people in their home away from home, though, Paul happened to connect with a few people that were his own type, people that he could relate to, people he could talk shop with because they were in the same business. It was tradition in the synagogue for people of the same trade to sit in groups in the synagogue, so by sitting with tentmakers, he would have met other tentmakers. In fact, this worked out really well for Paul because, as a foreigner, he didn't have a local distribution center or supply chain. Connecting with Aquila and Priscilla gave him a place to stay, supplies to do his work, and a local network to sell the tents he made. Life was good as a first-century tentmaking apostle in Corinth.

Even so, his heart was set on sharing the Gospel. Paul fulfilled his heart's desire in two ways. First, he discipled Aquila and Priscilla during his work. Second, he also took time on the Sabbath with Priscilla and Aquila to persuade Jews and Greeks of the truth of the Good News.

Keep in mind that this was the first-century when the idea of a forty-hour week hadn't been invented yet. Back in those days, weeks had 168 hours. I know. Crazy, right? People took a day of rest each week, but most of Paul's time can be assumed to have been spent making tents. It was through that time of making tents that he was making disciples.

One last piece of the puzzle is that tentmakers are sent. They are not just lone rangers serving the Lord without connection to a sending church. For Paul, this sending church was the church in Antioch:

While they were serving the Lord and fasting, the Holy Spirit said, "Set apart for me Barnabas and Saul [Paul] for the work to which I have called them." Then, after they had fasted and prayed and placed their hands on them, they sent them off.

Acts 13.2-3

So, Paul himself was commissioned and sent out by a church for his missionary journey as a tentmaker. It would be a mistake to think that we are better equipped than the Apostle Paul so that we could do this on our own.

Paul and Barnabas were also sent to different people than those of their home country. Acts 13 details how they started their journey going by way of Antioch's sister city, Seleucia, then on through Salamis and Paphos on Barnabas' home island of Cyprus; but those are cities they passed through on their way toward their real destination, which was the regions of Pamphylia, Pisidian, and Lycaonia. These regions were made up of people groups that were entirely different from Paul and Barnabas' home. The linguistic barriers they encountered led to animals nearly being sacrificed to Paul and Barnabas, who were thought to be gods (Acts 14). This certainly wouldn't have happened among their own people.

The point here is that this sending was not to their own people. To be a missionary is to be sent out by your own people to others for the purpose of sharing the Gospel.

Putting all of the pieces together of what a biblical tentmaker is, then, we can define the modern usage of tentmaker as "a person who is sent to use an occupation to live among and share the Good News with people who don't have it."

THE CASE FOR WORK

Work

I DON'T KNOW THAT we need a definition of work so much as we need a defense of work. There is a notion that work is a result of the Fall of Adam and part of the curse against him. If this is true, we shouldn't rejoice in the work we have to do, but we should rejoice in not doing any work. We should be happiest when we are lazy and bored. We should fight against every bit of work that is required of us as though it is a spiritual battle.

Fortunately for us, this isn't true. I say "fortunately" because the top cause of workplace frustration is not overwork but boredom and lack of purpose. When people use their gifts for a purpose they stand behind, they are fulfilled.

This is not just a logical conclusion, but it's a biblical conclusion. Before Adam's Fall and before any rule about forbidden fruit, Adam was given these commands:

> God blessed them and said to them, "Be fruitful and multiply! Fill the earth and subdue it! Rule over the fish of the sea and the birds of the air and every creature that moves on the ground."
>
> *Genesis 1.28*

> The Lord God took the man and placed him in the
> orchard in Eden to care for it and to maintain it.
>
> *Genesis 2.15*

Adam had a job before sin entered the world, so his
work at this job could not have been a result of sin entering the world.

Adam's purpose and the exercise of his gifting through an honest day's work was a blessing given to him before the Fall when the Lord said, "It is very good."

On the other hand, the curse on Adam for his part in
the Fall affects work:

> But to Adam he said, "Because you obeyed your wife
> and ate from the tree about which I commanded
> you, 'You must not eat from it,' cursed is the ground
> thanks to you; in painful toil you will eat of it all the
> days of your life. It will produce thorns and thistles
> for you, but you will eat the grain of the field. By
> the sweat of your brow you will eat food until you
> return to the ground, for out of it you were taken;
> for you are dust, and to dust you will return."
>
> *Genesis 3.17-19*

So, work was definitely affected by the Fall. Because of
the curse on the ground itself, work was made *much
more difficult* for Adam, but work itself was not a result
of the Fall. "Cursed ground," "painful toil," more "thorns

and thistles," and "sweat of [Adam's] brow" are the results of the Fall in relation to work. That being said, Adam's purpose and the exercise of his gifting through an honest day's work was a blessing given to him before the Fall when the Lord said, "It is very good."

This counters the philosophy that we should be happiest when we are lazy. In fact, laziness, or *sloth* to use an archaic term, is sin. God has given us a job to do and if we refuse to do it, we are in sin. We are most fulfilled and most delighted in God when we are doing the work he has given us to do.

So what about the common idea that you can only be fully satisfied in your work when you are following your passion? This idea is the notion that each of us has pre-existing passions, and unless our work fulfills them, our work itself will be unfulfilling.

The author Cal Newport comes down hard on this notion in his book *So Good They Can't Ignore You*. As part of that denunciation, he describes "Self-Determination Theory," which he attributes to being the closest scientific explanation to the real source of motivation, whether at work or elsewhere. Self-Determination Theory says the feeling of motivation comes from three things:[9]

1. Autonomy—the feeling that you have control over your day and that your actions are important

2. Competence—the feeling that you are good at what you do

3. Relatedness—the feeling of connectedness to other people

In addition, Newport cites a study by Amy Wrzesniewski regarding job satisfaction among college administrative assistants.[10] In roughly even measures, these administrative assistants described their work with these three definitions:

- It's a Job—It pays the bills.
- It's a Career—It is a path toward increasingly better work.
- It's a Calling—It is work that is an important part of my life and identity.

The surprising point of this even split is that it does not correlate to a sense of passion for administration that people had before their employment. Rather, it correlates directly to the length of time the administrative assistants had worked in the profession. In other words, those who felt it was just a job had worked the least amount of time, those who felt it was a career had worked somewhat longer, and those who described it as a calling had worked the longest. It is clear, then, that the more time you work in a particular trade, the more you feel it is your calling. Time helps develop autonomy, competence, and lasting connectedness with coworkers. Even non-faith-based scientific studies like Wrzesniewski's clearly indicate "working right trumps finding the right work"[11] as Newport summarizes. To describe it differently, faithfulness trumps passion.

Let me illustrate this point with my neighbor's story from a few years back. He repaired pallets out of his garage. Yes, that kind. The simple, wooden shipping pallets. Now, it is doubtful that anyone, even my neighbor, would have said when he was young, "I want to grow up to repair shipping pallets," or "I have a real passion for repairing shipping pallets." On the other hand, take a look at the ingenuity of my neighbor, and you will see that he was using an abundance of gifts he had been given to do this work.

First, he recognized the need. He learned through other factory work that shipments require pallets. Second, he recognized the supply. Many pallets in normal use get damaged. Next, he connected the supply to the demand. He collected used, broken pallets for free from businesses all around the city and would bring home about a hundred at a time. Next, he used physical labor and ingenuity to develop the tools for quickly disassembling the broken pallets, sorting the good pieces, and combining the pieces with others to make quality, handmade pallets that were even stronger than new ones. Finally, he used business acumen to sell them back to the shipping companies for no less than $20 each.

My neighbor had all of the ingredients for motivation mentioned above. He had complete autonomy over when he worked and how much he worked. He developed amazing competence to be able to identify pieces from broken pallet 'A' that he could use to fix broken pallet 'B,' and he did this exceptionally fast. In all, it took less than ten minutes to assemble a pallet that would sell for $20 with new nails being his only consumables. He cleared $120 per hour, and soon he had brothers and cousins and nephews that wanted to join him in his endeavor, which brought relatedness to others. He had all three elements of motivation from Self-Determination Theory, and he had no plans to change his work. Why would he?

This story illustrates from a very basic example that working right trumps finding the right work.

Rather than asking what your passion is, a better question might be, what needs to be done? Then, go do that. Just like my neighbor did.

Take another example. I am sure that a woman with the talents and heart of Mother Teresa could have applied herself to microeconomics and had a tremendous impact on lifting the people of India out of poverty. That was probably a greater need, and she would have had a greater physical impact on the people of India than what she ended up doing. Instead, she saw a need to help the destitute and dying. She saw a need to help people die with dignity, and she did something about it. It was a need that she identified, so she was fully committed to doing something about it.

Take Brother Lawrence as yet another example. Brother Lawrence was a monk born in France in 1610 who joined a monastery in Paris where he became the cook. He developed a habit which can only be described as practicing the presence of God.

> When Brother Lawrence began his work, he prayed to God, "O my God, since you are with me, and I must now, in obedience to your commands, apply my mind to these outward things, I ask you to grant me the grace to continue in your presence. Receive all my works, and possess all my desires." As he proceeded in his work, he continued his familiar conversation with his Maker, imploring His grace, and offering to Him all his actions.[12]

In this way, "Brother Lawrence felt it was a great delusion to think that the times of prayer ought to differ from other times."[12] Let me simplify a bit of the archaic language in this description. His work, even what many would consider menial drudgery of washing dishes, was a source of great delight and intimacy with God. He found that he was no more doing the work of God when he was at his monastic prayers than when he was cooking for his community. It's not about thinking that the "right job" for you lies just around the corner. Faithfulness trumps passion.

These three stories are not intended to be models for sharing the truth about Jesus. Rather, they model a biblical approach to work and confirm the biblical principle of Philippians 4.11 of being content in the state in which you are called and then working in it as to the Lord and not to men. This applied to all sorts of situations for the Apostle Paul. It applied to the financial state he was initially describing in Philippians 4, his state of hunger, his state of marriage (1 Corinthians 7), and certainly his state of employment. The point is not to think that you need to be doing something else in order to really serve the Lord, but instead to work heartily with contentment in the situation you are in.

To contrast those stories, let me use another story to illustrate giftedness for the work that needs to be done. My father-in-law was a Journeyman Electrician for most of his career. As he put in decade after decade of faithful work, his employer naturally presumed that he would want to be placed in a supervisory position. My father-in-law accepted the promotion, but an interesting thing happened.

Despite the seeming benefits of being a supervisor and having fewer direct work demands on him, my father-in-law chafed in this role. It simply wasn't in his make-up to manage others in his work. Night after night he would lie awake, nervous about how the job was going and whether others were going to fulfill their work diligently to prevent any loss to the company. At the end of a year, he was practically begging to have his old job back, doing the work himself rather than supervising others. Faithfulness trumps passion, especially when it is others who are telling you what to be passionate about. My father-in-law simply wanted to be faithful in his work without anyone else's presumptions about moving up the ladder of success.

So, you feel the Lord moving on your heart, and you want to serve him overseas. Don't feel that you have to give up your occupation, drop everything, and raise full support from friends and family in order to go overseas as a "full-time missionary." Use those skills, apprenticeships, certifications, degrees, and years of experience you might have—use your autonomy, competence, and connectedness—and serve the Lord among the unreached as a full-time missionary in the work you are in. Hard work is a dignified, honorable thing. You're listening to the wrong message if you feel you have no choice but to to abandon all of the hard work you've invested to serve the Lord in some other manner overseas. There is another way.

The Utilitarian Approach To Work

I wrote tongue in cheek earlier that the forty-hour week had not been invented yet. All humor aside, when was the forty-hour work week (or eight-hour work day) invented? As it happens, it has its origins in the Industrial Revolution of the late eighteenth century and early nineteenth century. The work day went through a progression from sixteen hours to twelve hours, then to ten hours, then to eight hours. Just prior to this progression, though, there was another related shift in society that launched the move to a forty-hour work week. The forty-hour work week was really a symptom of this societal change—the development of the firm or factory. This development came with the dissolution of craftsmanship.

Up to this point, a laborer worked in the craft that was usually what the whole family worked in. This craft was likely something that an individual's family had been working in and perfecting for generations. It could have been farming or it could have been metalworking or it could have been carpentry or it could have been masonry or it could have been shoemaking and the list goes on.

Those in the craft matured through the process as an apprentice first, then journeyman, then master craftsman. The important thing with these crafts and even agriculture is that these people worked with their own hands to provide for themselves. They owned whatever result came out and they had to bear the negative impact of any defects.

The establishment of the firm or the factory created a monumental shift in which people were now working for the benefit of someone else, namely, the owner of the factory. This massive shift to industrialization caused a massive shift in urbanization as well. People moved to cities because that is where they could acquire jobs that would provide them income to support themselves and their families.

Work became a utility, not a craft. Work's value was seen in what it could provide, not in the work itself.

That being the case, the entire family contributed to the work at the factory. It was not seen as strange for husbands, wives, and children to be working because they were all contributing to the income of the family in the same way that they had as craftsmen. Indeed, families wanted everyone to work so that they could earn more money to provide for the lifestyle benefits that they desired. Here is the key: work became a utility, not a craft. Work's value was seen in what it could provide, not in the work itself.

The impact of this change in work cannot be underestimated because it still thrives today for the vast majority of employees. This Utilitarian Approach to work thrived in the Twentieth Century American Dream leading to children asking,

"Why do I have to go to school?"

"So that you can get really smart."

"Why do I need to be really smart?"

"So that you can get good grades."

"Why do I need good grades?"

"So that you can get into college."

"Why do I need to go to college?"

"So that you can get a good job."

"Why do I need a good job?"

"So that you can raise a family."

"Why do I need to raise a family?"

"So that they can go to school. . . ."

You can see that this Utilitarian Approach to merely looking at work for what it can provide *strips work of its value and the greatest contribution that workers can make.* If you are simply a laborer in a transactional system of work for wages, you have stripped yourself of the valuable contribution you are specially gifted to make in the world.

Indeed, by extension, the Utilitarian Approach to work perpetuates the foundation of a sacred/secular divide. During the Industrial Revolution, it became evident that the Utilitarian Approach to work could be exploited against the workers. Classes of society such as the Proletariat and the Aristocracy were the natural outcomes of this societal change. The exploitation that followed was detrimental to the working class, so a move to fairly limit working hours each week protected the working class.

After all, they didn't have ownership of the outcome, so protection of the people became the foremost concern. The laborer's personal time away from work became sacred with weekly and periodic holidays, that is, holy days. Work became merely a secular endeavor to *occupy* oneself with, an *occup*ation.

The Intrinsic-Value Approach To Work

Contrast that with a view of work that embraces the value of the worker's contribution to the world through the work itself. The idea of an Intrinsic-Value Approach to work emphasizes the particular gift mix and abilities of the individual in the craft. No longer is the individual merely a time clock employee at the factory, but the individual represents a unique contribution that no one else can make. Of course, when this is exercised in an individual's craft as an apprentice, journeyman, and master, the individual's contribution to the outcome is obvious. When an incredibly ornate necklace is crafted by a silversmith, no one else could have made it exactly as that individual did. That being said, this sort of craft is now extremely rare, and it would be unrealistic to call for a return solely to craftsmanship.

Rather, *Work of Influence*, encouraged and motivated by the Book of Daniel, aligns itself with the many efforts of labor movements to *redeem the individual's contribution to the outcome of the work.* For example, business people, manufacturers, and software developers will immediately recognize process improvement movements such as Six Sigma, Lean Manufacturing, Kaizen, Agile Project Management, and Agile Development which. . . Human Resource teams will immediately recognize personality tests such as the Myers-Briggs Type Indicator, LIFO, and StrengthsFinder that are used to identify the unique, personal contribution employees can make in their trade. All of these approaches and principles buttress the individual's unique contribution to the end result.

Without the component of faith, it is impossible to recognize and reproduce God's design for work.

As such, these approaches begin to approximate the integration of faith and work expressed in the Book of Daniel, but—and this is key—*without the component of faith, it is impossible to recognize and reproduce God's design for work.* We see this in the New Testament with Paul's deep teaching on spiritual gifts and how each member contributes to the Church body, but we also see this in the individual example of Daniel whose faith and work were intricately entwined.

Daniel worked hard and excelled beyond all others. He did it because of his deep faith which he expressed whenever the Lord gave him opportunity. In short, he worked "as to the Lord and not to men."

Sacred Work, Sacred Mission

Earlier, I defined the modern usage of tentmaker as "a person who is sent to use their occupation to live among and share the Good News with people who don't have it." This definition notwithstanding, much of the discussion of this book applies to work in general, irrespective of where in the world that might occur.

Work is sacred. The lessons of Daniel speak to tentmakers, yes, but they speak powerfully to Joe the Plumber or whomever you may be. *Work of Influence* can be equally applied to faithful believers working hard at their jobs in their home countries. The principles of work apply here as well as there.

Dave Sable of Samaritan's Purse gave a powerful encouragement to this effect at a conference where he based his discussion on the following refrain:

> Whatever you are doing, work at it with enthusiasm, as to the Lord and not for people, because you know that you will receive your inheritance from the Lord as the reward. Serve the Lord Christ.
> *Colossians 3.23-24*

He continues, "Our work is honorable and holy because we serve the Lord Christ. . . . However, our purpose, reward, and significance is not tied to what goes on out there. Rather, as Christians, we find God's blessing in the sacredness of the work itself."[13]

Much of what I am writing here can be broadly applied to any work that followers of Jesus do. Even so, there are certain things that we learn from the life of Daniel that apply specifically to those who go overseas to work among the unreached. As such, this book will focus particularly on those aspects in the hope of seeing many readers take up the challenge of these incredible lives committed wholly to the most high God.

SECTION 2
COMMENTARY

DANIEL 1

The Real Battle

THE BOOK OF DANIEL is a very supernatural book. Sounds a bit odd to have to say that about a book of the Bible, doesn't it? Aren't all books of the Bible supernatural? Isn't it a bit redundant to say "very supernatural?" It either is or it isn't.

All books of the Bible have a supernatural origin, but there are books of the Bible that do emphasize the supernatural side of life more than others. For instance, Leviticus has supernatural parts, to be sure, but it is primarily a book of the Law for earthly order. Romans and Galatians, too, have deeply supernatural portions, but they are primarily logical treatises of the mind.

The book of Daniel, on the other hand, concerns itself from beginning to end with the supernatural realm. We've got miracles and dreams and visions and divine graffiti and strange people popping into fires like popcorn. It's inescapable. The book is all about the interplay between the spiritual world and the physical world, and in this way, it speaks reams about tentmaking.

Principle 1
Tentmaking Is a Spiritual Battle

The book launches in:

> In the third year of the reign of King Jehoiakim of
> Judah, King Nebuchadnezzar of Babylon advanced
> against Jerusalem and laid it under siege.
> *Daniel 1.1*

From the very first verse of the very first chapter, this
book is a spiritual power struggle. It's not as obvious
to the modern reader, but at the time when Daniel was
writing, most cities and regions had their own gods
that were worshiped. Moving your family to a new city
usually meant worshiping a new god and that meant
learning all of the intricacies of serving this god. When
cities started chucking rocks at each other, that meant
that the gods of those cities were also at war. The god
of the city that won was obviously stronger since it had
helped gain the victory. So, to the original audience,
Daniel 1.1 was an introduction to the spiritual power
struggle between the gods of Nebuchadnezzar and the
God of Jehoiakim.

In this particular case, the God of the King of Judah must have obviously been thought to be weaker
than the god of the Babylonians. After all, the Babylonians were victorious. Their favorite god Nebo was
celebrated in a spiritual victory by Nebuchadnezzar.
Most certainly, this god's namesake, Nebuchadnezzar,
was thinking he was the big kid on the block, a force
to be reckoned with.

This is the question for the tentmaker: Is it any different today? No! As you explore the idea of tentmaking,

you are already in a spiritual battle. This battle will continue until you leave the host land you've decided to go to, and maybe longer. The Enemy wants to do whatever is necessary to prevent your faithful witness of the Good News among these people.

As tentmakers in the Arabian Gulf, my wife and I befriended a family shortly before the husband went on Hajj in Mecca. It is customary for travelers to bring gifts home to family and friends, so our friend gave us holy water and prayer beads from Mecca.

We accepted the gifts politely, but afterward we were torn as to what we should do with them. We didn't want to seem ungrateful or disrespectful, so we just tucked them into a corner.

Over the next weeks, my wife and I began having very strange, negative events happen to us. We began to get sick repeatedly, things began to break down in our home, and frightful nightmares plagued our sleep. We sought counsel from another tentmaker couple, and our dear friend Ruth prayed with us for discernment. After concluding our prayer, she asked if there was any foothold that the Enemy might have in our home, such as a religious object or something that might give the Enemy a means into our lives. Without hesitation, we identified the holy water and prayer beads from Mecca. Immediately after casting them out of our home, the sicknesses went away, the strange negative coincidences stopped happening, and the nightmares were cut off. We live in a spiritual world, and we have a spiritual enemy that is not happy when tentmakers enter his territory.

Understanding, then, that it is a spiritual battle you are engaging in as a tentmaker, I encourage you to pray for the regimes that govern the country you are aiming to live in. In fact, recognizing the battle we are in, I urge you to pray for the regimes of the world hotspots even now, even if you are not aiming to go there. Do you pray for North Korea? Do you pray for Afghanistan and Pakistan? Do you pray for Russia and Saudi Arabia and Syria and China? It is a spiritual battle we are waging, and we can contribute powerfully by praying well in advance of the days we are even in our tentmaking roles.

The point of Daniel 1.1 is that countries and peoples believed that the gods that were worshiped determined the victory. In Daniel's case, when we read of Israel's defeat, Babylon believed that the Israelite God, Yahweh, was weak and inferior to the god Nebo.

> Now the Lord delivered King Jehoiakim of Judah into [Nebuchadnezzar's] power, along with some of the vessels of the temple of God. He brought them to the land of Babylonia to the temple of his god and put the vessels in the treasury of his god.
>
> *Daniel 1.2*

To rub salt in the wound, so to speak, the artifacts that were used for the worship of Yahweh were taken from Yahweh's place of worship in the temple to the Babylonian temple of Nebo and used for worship of this god instead. This is clearly an act of spiritual defiance of the God of Judah. So, the book of Daniel starts with the people of Israel being hopelessly overrun by the Babylonians and the Almighty God being deeply insulted. Hopelessness and despair set the stage. The cast is introduced. Incredible events now unfold, leading to proclamation after proclamation of the great and Almighty God.

Principle 2
God Is in Control

As a tentmaker, you will walk through times of deep despair, and it might even be in "Verse 1" of your overseas adventure. You and your family will undoubtedly go through culture shock, wondering what God was thinking in calling you to the nations. What has God done, uprooting you from your home land and dropping you in this new cultural, linguistic, and religious milieu with serious occupational hazards to navigate? Daniel can relate to all of that. When you are walking through your Verse 1, take courage that the God of Verse 2 is still God over Verse 1.

Take a look at the way verse 2 starts:

> Now the Lord delivered King Jehoiakim of Judah into [Nebuchadnezzar's] power. . . .

You might be thinking, *How is that better than verse one? It says King Jehoiakim was captured along with all of Judah!* It's better in this way: "Now the Lord . . . ." God did it. This hopeless situation that Judah was going through, this enslavement and deportation of its people, came from the Father's hand. It wasn't an accident; it wasn't because God was weak; it wasn't because Babylon had more military prowess; and it certainly wasn't because Nebo was more powerful. Daniel sets the stage for the whole book by noting that God delivered Judah into the hand of the Babylonians.

This is a real challenge for many people because they don't like to think that God would allow bad things to happen to his people. The fact of the matter is, God did just that and he still does just that. Through it all, we have this encouragement from the New Testament:

And we know that all things work together for good for those who love God, who are called according to his purpose.

Romans 8.28

Bad things will happen in life whether that life is lived as a tentmaker overseas like Paul or whether it is lived in the comforts of your hometown. For those who trust God and are walking according to their calling, there is a purpose even behind those bad things. You can be sure that God isn't allowing these things out of spite or to be unkind. Rather, he has a purpose in all things to mold and shape us into the people of faith that he wants us to be. It is a striking step of faith, but when bad things happen, ask God, "Father, what is it you want to teach me in this experience?" Let me illustrate this with a personal story.

In 1993, I spent a semester abroad studying in Cairo, Egypt, and my study program had two rules. First, don't talk about religion. Second, don't talk about politics.

As students, we could do a lot even under those rules, such as seeing the tourist sites, getting to know the history of the country, and even visiting fancy coffee shops like we were in the habit of doing. But, after eight weeks of abiding by these rules, I realized that they were more restrictive than even the laws of the Egyptian government which allowed people to talk about their religion if they were asked. I wasn't even doing this.

On the evening of October 26, I attended a church service with my good friend, an Egyptian Christian. Our group of American students had noticed a fancy coffee shop the night before at the Semiramis Hotel that I thought would make a good meeting place. I wanted to ask my friend how I could wisely share my faith without being dangerous or looking for trouble. After the church service, we walked the half hour to the Semiramis Hotel, and he shared all of the ways I could wisely share my faith. I was encouraged beyond measure.

As we approached the hotel, he felt like he wanted to go home and skip coffee, so we stood across the street from the hotel. He got his bus to Heliopolis, and I started my half hour walk back to Zamalek. Only moments later, I noticed two ambulances racing toward me. Curious, I thought, "That's odd. I've never seen any ambulances in Cairo before. It must be someone pretty important."

The next morning, the director of our program began class instead of our instructor and announced, "I suppose you better hear from me and not from the newspapers or something else. Last night, a man walked into the Semiramis Hotel coffee shop shouting, 'Allahu akbar! Allahu akbar!' 'God is great! God is great!' He then shot all the Westerners he could see, killing three and critically wounding three others."

I was simply stunned. My friend and I had been walking to that coffee shop. Instead of going in for coffee, which would have almost certainly cost my life, we stood across the street waiting for his bus because he just didn't "feel" like going in for coffee.

So many times in our lives we are protected by God, but we just don't realize it. This was one of those times when God pulled back the blinds and showed me his protection much like he did for Gehazi, Elisha's servant, of the Old Testament.

> The prophet's attendant got up early in the morning. When he went outside there was an army surrounding the city, along with horses and chariots. He said to Elisha, "Oh no, my master! What will we do?" He replied, "Don't be afraid, for our side

outnumbers them." Then Elisha prayed, "O Lord, open his eyes so he can see." The Lord opened the servant's eyes and he saw that the hill was full of horses and chariots of fire all around Elisha.

2 Kings 6.15-17

My Cairo incident taught me in vivid color this simple principle,

The safest place to be is in the will of God.

The most dangerous place to be is out of the will of God.

By safe, it doesn't mean that nothing bad will happen. Rather, it means that whatever does happen is from the Father's hand. He has a purpose in it.

If you are walking out of the will of God, you are in a dangerous place. Consult with Ananias and Sapphira if you are wondering about this (Acts 5).

The safest place to be is in the will of God. The most dangerous place to be is out of the will of God.

I say this again because it is critical to your faith as a tentmaker. You need to get this principle right because without it, you will land in a pit of resentment, anger, and self-pity when bad things happen. Rather than hating God for taking you across the globe and allowing difficulties to happen that would not have happened in your home country, you can turn to your loving Father in faith and ask, "What is it, Lord, that I need to learn from this? How do you want to shape my faith by this situation? How are you going to work this for good for me, Lord? What is my take away?"

Even if you never see all of the reasons the Lord allows tragedy or difficulty, you can trust that his purpose is in it.

Principle 3
Go to the Places of Greatest Need

Did you ever think of the story of Daniel taking place in modern-day Iraq? Does it put it into a different perspective when you think of a Jew being captured in Israel, transported 1000 miles around the desert through Syria, and put into slavery in Iraq?

> The king commanded Ashpenaz, who was in charge of his court officials, to choose some of the Israelites who were of royal and noble descent— young men in whom there was no physical defect and who were handsome, well versed in all kinds of wisdom, well educated and having keen insight, and who were capable of entering the king's royal service— and to teach them the literature and language of the Babylonians.
>
> *Daniel 1.3-4*

To be sure, the Babylonians (Iraqis) were not considered the people of God. The Jews held that title for themselves, so the Jews would have been considered "reached" with the message of God. On the other hand, the Babylonians qualified as an Unreached People Group then just as the Iraqis do in modern day Iraq.

But we do have to answer an obvious question, "Come on, can we really compare a slave in ancient Babylon to a modern day tentmaker among an Unreached People Group?"

To answer this question, let me state that this book affirms strongly the integration of faith and work. This principle is taught throughout the Bible for both missionaries who are sent and for others who do the sending. Take a look at a few of the passages that teach this.

Commit your works to the Lord, and your plans will be established.

Proverbs 16.3

There is nothing better for people than to eat and drink, and to find enjoyment in their work. I also perceived that this ability to find enjoyment comes from God.

Ecclesiastes 2.24

And whatever you do in word or deed, do it all in the name of the Lord Jesus, giving thanks to God the Father through him.

Colossians 3.17

[Show] yourself to be an example of good works in every way. In your teaching show integrity, dignity, and a sound message that cannot be criticized, so that any opponent will be at a loss, because he has nothing evil to say about us.

Titus 2.7-8

You yourselves know that these hands of mine provided for my needs and the needs of those who were with me. By all these things, I have shown you that by working in this way we must help the weak, and remember the words of the Lord Jesus that he himself said, "It is more blessed to give than to receive."

Acts 20.34-35

That is just a quick sampling of Scripture passages that underscore the deep integration between faith and work. Don't miss this: your work ethic reflects your faith epic. The value you place on work is part of your faith story.

So, let me ask you, of all of those verses above, which of them is nullified for slaves? Are slaves exempt from working "as to the Lord and not to men?" Did Paul give the slave Onesimus a "pass" on working heartily in the book of Philemon?

Your work ethic reflects your faith epic. The value you place on work is part of your faith story.

Of course not. Rather, Paul sent this runaway slave back to his master *to work for his master as a slave.* Paul could have declared Onesimus free because his master Philemon owed Paul so much. Or, he could have simply sent a letter to Philemon saying, "I'm keeping Onesimus here to work with me. I know you will agree that this is the right thing to do."

No. Paul sent Onesimus back to work as a slave under the authority of Philemon, and this model is clear indication that Paul expected slaves to share this mindset of integration of faith and work.

To punctuate this notion, Paul sent the following instructions to the believers in the region of Ephesus and used this instruction to slaves to establish normative behavior for all believers:

> Slaves, obey your human masters with fear and trembling, in the sincerity of your heart as to Christ, not like those who do their work only when someone is watching—as people pleasers—but as slaves of Christ doing the will of God from the heart. Obey with enthusiasm, as though serving the Lord and not people, because you know that each person, whether slave or free, if he does something good, this will be rewarded by the Lord.
>
> *Ephesians 6.5-7*

The fact that Daniel and his three friends were slaves certainly doesn't absolve them from obeying all of the instructions of Scripture about work. No one is condoning any form of slavery here, but even though they may not have had the specifics of Paul's instructions, the principle is timeless.

Principle 4
Do Not Think More Highly of Yourself than You Ought, or "Humility and How I Attained It"

The king commanded Ashpenaz, who was in charge of his court officials, to choose some of the Israelites who were of royal and noble descent— young men in whom there was no physical defect and who were handsome, well versed in all kinds of wisdom, well educated and having keen insight, and who were capable of entering the king's royal service—and to teach them the literature and language of the Babylonians. . . .

When the time appointed by the king arrived, the overseer of the court officials brought them into Nebuchadnezzar's presence. When the king spoke with them, he did not find among the entire group anyone like Daniel, Hananiah, Mishael, or Azariah. So they entered the king's service.

Daniel 1.3-4, 18-19

This was the beginning of Daniel's friendship in the community with Ashpenaz. We haven't seen Daniel offering persuasive arguments for Ashpenaz to convert to Judaism, and as much as we can tell, Daniel wasn't distributing The Four Spiritual Laws to Ashpenaz. Even so, Ashpenaz was able to recognize something different, something outstanding in Daniel and his three friends Hananiah, Azariah, and Mishael. Now, we do read that Daniel and his three friends were of royal or noble descent, but that wasn't enough in itself to distinguish these gentlemen from everyone else. Presumably, there were more than four young men of royal and noble descent that were captured, so something else made them stand out from the others.

Here are some of the qualities recorded about Daniel and his friends:

- They had no physical defects.
- They were handsome.
- They were well versed in all kinds of wisdom already.
- They were well educated.
- They had keen insight.

These are the qualities that made them "capable of entering the king's royal service."

Merely by writing this, Daniel was in a bit of a pickle. On the one hand, Daniel would have been aware of Scriptures that explain he is not supposed to puff himself up.

> The fear of the Lord is to hate evil;
> I hate arrogant pride and the evil way
> and perverse utterances.
>
> *Proverbs 8.13*

> When pride comes, then comes disgrace,
> but with humility comes wisdom.
>
> *Proverbs 11.2*

> The Lord abhors every arrogant person;
> rest assured that they will not go unpunished.
>
> *Proverbs 16.5*

> Pride goes before destruction,
> and a haughty spirit before a fall.
>
> *Proverbs 16.18*

This was serious business. Daniel was not supposed to be proud and arrogant. Of all the qualities and attributes a faithful follower of the law is supposed to have, self-exaltation is not one of them. Yet, it was Daniel who wrote all of these great things about himself. How does that reflect a humble attitude?

In your life as a tentmaker, you will encounter something very similar. For example, when you recount your credentials and successes and work history in your *Curriculum Vitae*, how do you do this without pride? When you share an innovation with your superior that will save the company $10 million each year, how is that not boastful? When you submit an annual report that lists the seven innovations that have revolutionized your classroom, how will you do that without seeming arrogant to your jealous coworkers?

Of all the qualities and attributes a faithful follower of the law is supposed to have, self-exaltation is not one of them.

We can see from Daniel a good pattern to protect our own humility while also telling the story. It is true, Daniel lists all of these qualities of exceptional praise and he even says further on that his advice and answers exceeded the value of all of his compatriots. Nonetheless, Daniel does not continue to inflate and build on those aspects. He doesn't circle back again and again and again in a boastful way. Sure, these points are part of his story, but his simple way of telling them as part of his story is humble, not boastful. In order to tell how he got an audience with the king, he has to share some of the qualifications and the elimination process that the king's service entailed. To share how he impacted the king's thinking through his counsel, Daniel has to share why the king prefered his advice above others.

In fact, it is through Daniel's humble approach that relationship doors are opened up for him and his three friends.

Daniel was not the subject of a democratic election where he had to curry favor with everyone on every issue in order to glean votes. Daniel was not seeking the company of great ones. He was not targeting the high court. Daniel had no idea that he would actually serve in the king's service. To be sure, it was a long shot for any one of the Jews to outshine the Babylonian young men who were vying for these positions. As for Daniel, he just faithfully did what he always did. The rest was up to God.

There's something that we can gather from the effect of Daniel's faithfulness, though. Daniel was building relational capital. Daniel came into this gig as a brilliant, good-looking, well-educated young man. Oh, and did I mention he was brilliant? If you can impress the world's most powerful king and all of his administrators, your mama did something right. Nevertheless, he didn't rely on that brilliance alone. He built and used relational capital.

Principle 5
You Cannot Serve God and Yen

Daniel had built up a lot of relational capital with good old Ashpenaz. Even so, in 2.14-16 we see he had built up this relational capital with Arioch as well and even the king.

> Then Daniel spoke with prudent counsel to Arioch, who was in charge of the king's executioners and who had gone out to execute the wise men of Babylon. He inquired of Arioch the king's deputy, "Why is the decree from the king so urgent?" Then Arioch informed Daniel about the matter. So Daniel went in and requested the king to grant him time, that he might disclose the interpretation to the king.
>
> *Daniel 2.14-16*

Even with this relational capital with Arioch, Daniel didn't use it for his own self-aggrandizement, which was the real proof in the pudding of his humility. Instead of boldly asking Arioch and the king for more time, he could have served his own purposes with his relational capital. Daniel had it made. He could have been a fat (literally) cat with all of the best foods and comforts that Babylon had to offer. Even so, his integrity was more important than his comfort. He used his influence to proclaim the truth of God's supremacy time and again. He used this influence for the next seventy to eighty years.

His integrity was more important than his comfort. He used his influence to proclaim the truth of God's supremacy time and again.

As a tentmaker, the potential will be there to make money—a lot of money. Living expenses go down, salaries go up, and in some cases, taxes disappear. The potential is there to make a lot of money, but what will you do with it? In your host country, you will almost certainly be in a position of influence. When I was working with youth in Bahrain in the Arabian Gulf, one of the Indian youth explained very bluntly, "If you were Indian, I wouldn't listen to you. I listen to you because you are American." So much for my ego of being a great teacher! Like it or not, you will be in a position of influence, so what will you do with it?

It's common for tentmakers to get paid 30% more (it's not unheard of to be paid 500% more) working in the same job overseas than in their home countries. It's common for companies to include airfare to your home country every year for your entire family. It's common to include housing. Sometimes, contracts even include a car or a car and a driver.

How would you use that income? After all, it is a lot like Daniel's "royal delicacies and royal wine." You could certainly consume it. After all, you earned it, right? You could live large and enjoy it.

Let me paint another picture for you from Scripture. Paul is speaking to the Corinthian believers who were living large with lots of money, so he questions them,

> What do you have that you did not receive? And if you received it, why do you boast as though you did not? Already you are satisfied! Already you are rich! You have become kings without us!
>
> *1 Corinthians 4.7b-8a*

It was obvious to any observer that the people of Corinth were rich. They were living large. In spite of that, Paul is pressing the reset button to point out that everything they had was a gift. They shouldn't be living like boastful kings, consuming the riches they made when their riches were actually a gift from God. When things are going well and bills are being paid and the savings account is growing, it is a gift. His stern warning to tentmakers (and anyone else with money to spare) is that you should not boast as though you have made all of this money through your own power and you didn't receive it as a gift. 1 Corinthians is a very emotional book for Paul, the tentmaker, because he labored so as not to be a burden to the Corinthian church. In the face of Paul's sacrifice, the Corinthians continued living the good life, consuming their wealth. Paul uses that backdrop to teach that *some Christian workers should be supported* by the church (1 Corinthians 9) and the Corinthian church should be using their wealth to support them. To reinforce that point, Paul ends the book with specific instructions to numerous churches to take up a regular collection in the church so that those resources can be distributed for foreign relief work of the worldwide Church.

> With regard to the collection for the saints, please follow the directions that I gave to the churches of Galatia: On the first day of the week, each of you should set aside some income and save it to the extent that God has blessed you, so that a collection will not have to be made when I come. Then, when I arrive, I will send those whom you approve with letters of explanation to carry your gift to Jerusalem.
>
> *1 Corinthians 16.1-3*

Consider next that Paul spent all of 1 Corinthians 9 clarifying that even though he chose not to take money, he could have rightfully done so as a Christian worker. *Some* Christian workers should receive financial support. The obvious point is to give to those workers to support them.

Some Christian workers should receive financial support. The obvious point is to give to those workers to support them.

Finally, Paul says that as a routine practice, churches should be taking up a collection to redistribute wealth to needy churches elsewhere. The bottom line is this, they shouldn't be living like boastful kings, consuming the riches they made when their riches were actually a gift from God.

So, what are you going to do with the "king's delicacies" entrusted to you?

Principle 6
Your Work Has Intrinsic Value

This principle of tentmaking that we draw from the book of Daniel is, perhaps, the most profound and most revolutionary of this book. Though this principle isn't expressly stated in the words of Daniel, it, nonetheless, becomes clear when we understand the context of the story. To do that, we have to put ourselves into Daniel's shoes. These men were:

> young men in whom there was no physical defect and who were handsome, well versed in all kinds of wisdom, well educated and having keen insight, and who were capable of entering the king's royal service—and [were taught] the literature and language of the Babylonians.
>
> *Daniel 1.4*

As was mentioned earlier, Daniel could have been on the cover of GQ Babylon, if there was such a thing. He was handsome, he was young, and he was fit with a perfect body with no defect. The same could be said for his three friends Hananiah, Azariah, and Mishael. They had everything going for them. They could have just sat back and enjoyed their status, sipping piña coladas or something.

However, along with being "well versed in all kinds of wisdom, well educated and having keen insight," these guys had a work ethic that was deeply ingrained in them through the Hebrew education of the Bible. All of the teachings of Moses, the works of history, the Psalms and Proverbs that point to the value of work were part of their makeup. It simply was not in their nature to rest on their laurels. This expressed their deep commitment to the intrinsic value of work.

Consider this example that Moses recorded in Exodus 36:

So Bezalel and Oholiab and every skilled person in whom the Lord has put skill and ability to know how to do all the work for the service of the sanctuary are to do the work according to all that the Lord has commanded.

Moses summoned Bezalel and Oholiab and every skilled person in whom the Lord had put skill— everyone whose heart stirred him to volunteer to do the work, and they received from Moses all the offerings the Israelites had brought to do the work for the service of the sanctuary, and they still continued to bring him a freewill offering each morning.

Exodus 36.1-3

At the very least, Jewish education consisted of memorizing Moses' writings in the first five books of the Bible. This passage would have been ready in the minds of these young men at a moment's notice. Reciting it would have caused their chests to well with joy as they considered the work ethic of Bezalel and Oholiab.

That being said, read carefully how these men and every skilled person got their skill: "Bezalel and Oholiab and every skilled person in whom the Lord had put skill—everyone whose heart stirred him to volunteer to do the work . . . ." The Lord put this skill in them. The Lord enabled them to do their work with the utmost care. The Lord was the one who both benefited from the beautiful craftsmanship that was exhibited and the one who put it there to begin with. The work was not about merely getting a job done. It was about making a contribution to the world through the skill that God himself had put in these people.

Another passage that relates a similar idea comes from just a few chapters earlier in this instruction from God to Moses:

> You must make holy garments for your brother Aaron, for glory and for beauty.
>
> *Exodus 28.2*

This passage, too, would have been familiar to Daniel when he thought of what sort of work he would aspire to. God's instruction makes clear that it was not just about getting a job done. He didn't say, "Yeah, I suppose you should make some clothes for Aaron and his sons." The craftsmanship that the Lord required was nothing short of glorious and beautiful.

So, when we read about Daniel and his friends, recognize that this is the concept of workmanship, craftsmanship, and work ethic that they strove to measure up to. In fact, you could say that their work ethic reflected their faith epic. The Jewish culture was a culture that respected the Intrinsic Value of work.

In this case, these young men were already recognized as brilliant. They were smart enough to serve in the king's royal service. Note that at this time, the king's royal service was based on merit and brilliance, not on popularity. Today's political populism wouldn't have passed muster with Nebuchadnezzar. There were no second chances. As we will see, if your advice or abilities did not meet the king's standard of excellence, you were dispatched, to put it nicely.

Daniel and his friends were seen as brilliant, but then, add on to that brilliance three years of intensive training in the "language and literature" of the Babylonians. After that training, these men would have been congratulated with an acceptable level of service to the king, but it wasn't enough for them. *These young men were ten times smarter and better than everyone else* in every matter of wisdom and insight (Daniel 1.20). This does not happen by accident. It happens through an incredible amount of hard work and the blessing of the Lord over and above that hard work. So yes, their intrinsic work ethic was part of their intrinsic faith epic.

Principle 7
Read Everything

As a college student, I simply ate up my archeology and anthropology classes with Professor Russ Lunak. I couldn't get enough of them. One of the lessons I learned from Professor Lunak was simply this: Read everything about the people you are going to. Wow. Read everything? Yes. Everything.

In that regard, I suppose that going to the unreached has one thing going for it if you're not fond of reading. For many of these people groups, there is very little written, which makes your reading task easier. In fact, for some of the people groups, you might be the first person to go to them from the Western world. Even so, it seemed like Daniel followed this principle through three years of intensive study and preparation among the people with whom he was working. Daniel and his friends were

> young men in whom there was no physical defect and who were handsome, well versed in all kinds of wisdom, well educated and having keen insight, and who were capable of entering the king's royal service—and [were taught] the literature and language of the Babylonians. So the king assigned them a daily ration from his royal delicacies and from the wine he himself drank. They were to be trained for the next three years. At the end of that time they were to enter the king's service.
>
> *Daniel 1.4-5*

Often, people begrudge the fact that they have to learn the language of the host culture. They have no lack of excuses for not learning the language such as being too old or being able to say all they need to in English or not being good at learning languages or being a "visual learner" even when the language is only a spoken language. Let me put this plainly: these are all excuses, not reasons. My graduate degree is in linguistics, and I can firmly say that there are approaches to help every learner acquire a new language. If you want to know more, my email is at the end of the book.

That being said, if my word isn't enough for you, take Daniel as an example. These few verses say that he spent three years learning the language and literature of the Babylonians, but what did that include?

To begin with, Daniel's first language would have been Hebrew which he would have spoken in his home and would have read in literature since he was "well versed" and "well educated." Daniel's second language would have been the trade language, namely Aramaic, which would have also been spoken in Babylon. This is the language he would have used to relate to Ashpenaz and, eventually, King Nebuchadnezzar. Daniel even writes portions of his book in Aramaic rather than Hebrew when he is addressing content to a broader audience.

Daniel's third and fourth languages would have been Sumerian and Akkadian, two dead languages that, nonetheless, contained the history of the Babylonians in their cuneiform script. This cuneiform script in the Sumerian language is the oldest written language on earth. It was formed by pressing a wedge-shaped end of a reed into clay tablets before letting the tablets dry in the hot, Iraqi sun. These tablets were all the rage and were cool enough to make any iPad jealous.

Daniel, then, had the ability to understand the oldest language on earth right up to understanding the hipster Aramaic that was for everyone in-the-know in 605 B.C. Excuses aside, Daniel was a serious student of language.

What did the literature of the Babylonians include? It certainly included the things that Daniel was adept at, which were visions and dreams according to verse 17, but it would have also included what "wise men, astrologers, magicians, or diviners" studied (2.27). In other words, the education of Daniel and his three friends would have included all of these different disciplines. Daniel would have been an expert in astrology, magic, and divination as well as general wisdom.

That idea is hard to wrap my mind around. In my educational background I've read some literature as requirements of classes that has put horrible images in my mind. It was hard to read, but to some extent, I see the purpose of being exposed to that literature because it exposes the true nature of human sin. Daniel, on the other hand, had spells and incantations as part of his required reading. Even through this, the Lord was able to protect his mind so that he wasn't tempted or drawn into these spells. In the same way, when you are exposed to literature of your host culture that you would otherwise oppose, pray for the Lord's discernment and protection in the midst of it.

One would think that this vast accumulation of knowledge itself would be a feat amazing enough. But Babylon was not a research institute where these young men could simply do their thing and amass tremendous knowledge. Rather, they had to synthesize that knowledge for the benefit of the king, to summarize and share their brilliance with people who could not operate on their level of brilliance.

Dr. Mark Muska, one of my college professors, summarized the interplay between knowledge and wisdom. Recognizing that knowledge is the mere accumulation of facts, he said wisdom is "knowledge applied to skillful living."[14] If you are foolish about your knowledge, you are not wise. For example, if a genius theoretical physicist says in his heart, "There is no God," he is showing himself to be a fool, not wise (Psalm 14.1). Wisdom takes that knowledge and applies it to skillful living.

Wisdom is "knowledge applied to skillful living."

That will often be the case in tentmaking as well. Consider that you as a tentmaker will be coming with your home country knowledge, you'll be diving into the host country knowledge, and you will be an expert in the specialty knowledge related to your job. Your role will be to synthesize your areas of knowledge into usable pieces of information for consumption by others who do not have that knowledge. Your value will be in communicating exceptionally well, both in your employment and in your witness. Take the time and spend the effort to improve both your verbal and written communications skills.

As an interesting side effect of this vast amount of "knowledge work" that Daniel was involved in, it is worth noting that he was in his 80s or possibly his 90s when he wrote the book of Daniel. He seems to have no problem recalling details like names and facts from his early teen years. There seems to be no sign of dementia in this man. Perhaps it is on account of this knowledge work that he was able to keep his mental faculties strong even into his advanced years.

Principle 8
Major on the Majors

But the overseer of the court officials renamed them. He gave Daniel the name Belteshazzar, Hananiah he named Shadrach, Mishael he named Meshach, and Azariah he named Abednego.

But Daniel made up his mind that he would not defile himself with the royal delicacies or the royal wine. He therefore asked the overseer of the court officials for permission not to defile himself.

Daniel 1.7-8

This presents an interesting dilemma that we might not fully understand when approaching the situation from a Western cultural perspective. As a bit of background, there are a few names for the God that was worshiped by Daniel, Hananiah, Azariah, and Mishael. In fact, those names are embedded in the names of each of these young men. Wherever you see the suffix -el or -jah, you know this is a reference to the one, true God. That being the case, the Babylonians didn't appreciate the names of God being embedded into the names of their slaves, so the overseer of the court officials gave each of them names with Babylonian gods embedded into them, specifically Bel-, -ach and -nego.

In my cultural context, this seems like a big deal and a direct offense. My name is David Cross. If someone decided to nickname me David Crescent to give me a Muslim nickname or they called me Mr. Shiva as a Hindu nickname, I would not take well to it. Even so, these four servants didn't have a problem with it. Sure, they wouldn't have chosen the names themselves, but as my wife says, it was like water off a duck's back. They let it go.

On the other hand, Daniel had a very different view of the royal delicacies and royal wine that was presented to him. He (and subsequently, his friends) saw that eating and drinking of the delicacies would "defile" these men. They recognized that something about eating and drinking was obviously very different from even nicknames that included polytheistic divinities. They had evidently spent considerable time thinking this through because, to be blunt, their lives were on the line with what they asked.

So, what was the big deal about the food and drink anyway? Much has been made of the notion that they were asking to be vegetarians. People take this to mean that this must be biblical evidence that a vegetarian lifestyle is superior to that of eating meat. To the contrary, we infer that it was a divine miracle that these men remained healthy and even stronger than others from just vegetables and water. They simply weren't getting all the necessary nutrients, but God still came through for them and kept them healthy *in spite of* their limited diet. That's why this miracle was included by Daniel.

Ceremonially clean Jews would have had no problem with properly prepared beef or goat or lamb, so why would they have insisted on not having any meat? Even if they could have refused certain foods such as pork, why did they make an issue over all meat? Some people suggest that perhaps the meats were mixed with ceremonially clean and unclean animals, but then how do we explain the wine?

Culturally, we know that animals were sacrificed in the name of deities and a portion of wine was poured out as a libation to the Babylonian gods. By that measure, *all meat and wine* was dedicated to these polytheistic deities. To consume it would defile Daniel and his friends. On the other hand, vegetables were not "slaughtered" in the name of Bel and water was not poured out to Nebo. They were safe.

So what are we to make of the difference between the issue of the names and the issue of the foods? Were these four men contextualizing the message of the one God that they served? Were they changing the message to make it more palatable to those who might object? No, this wasn't contextualization. They weren't changing the message. Instead, they were choosing the best place to communicate the truth they had to bear. As far as nicknames they might have been called? Call them what you want. That's something outside of themselves that will not defile them.

They weren't changing the message. Instead, they were choosing the best place to communicate the truth they had to bear.

On the other hand, they were convicted that taking sacrificed food into their bodies was defiling, and they could not concede. They had a message to bear, namely, that the God they served was superior, that "Heaven rules" (Daniel 4.26). They picked their battles and chose food as a place to make that message clear.

The principle for tentmakers, then, is to use that deep study referred to earlier to learn all you can about the best place to communicate truth. For example, Don Richardson has written an entire book identifying cultural stories that introduce people to the concept of a supreme God.[15] Knowing those stories and the inroads to the Gospel for your host culture can be key to the success among those people.

Principle 9
Be Audacious

In the West, many people look at the idea of favors as soft bribes and a single stroke away from corruption. That's a pretty harsh outlook, but it doesn't have to be perceived this way. From my experience, for example, most people don't necessarily keep a ledger of accounts where they think, "David owes me one, so I'll call it in now." There may be instances of that, but largely, it is more relational. People respond with generosity to help you out as your friend. They see this as what friends do for one another. As their friend, they know that you will do the same when the time comes. The point is, favors are much more relational, less transactional, and less corrupt than might be assumed.

As an example of this sort of favor that is not a bribe, let me share what my friend Faisal did for our family. While we lived in Oman, my wife started having problems with teenage boys harassing her when she was walking on the street. Not only would they yell obscenities at her, but they rode their motorbikes directly at her to drive her off the road as she was walking.

I mentioned this problem to my friend Faisal who was a member of the police force and was home visiting from his station about 400 km away. I wanted to know what I should do and how we should handle it. He immediately asked me what their names were. When I said that I did not know, he instructed us to ask their names, in fact, ask their father's name, then we should tell Faisal. I countered, "But Faisal, you'll be 400 km away. What can you do?" He cut me short, saying, "I'll take care of it. Don't worry about it. I'll take care of it."

Faisal was willing to ask for favors to help a friend even from hundreds of kilometers away because that's what friends do.

Daniel's time had come to cash in on some of that relational capital.

> Then God made the overseer of the court officials sympathetic to Daniel. But he responded to Daniel, "I fear my master the king. He is the one who has decided your food and drink. What would happen if he saw that you looked malnourished in comparison to the other young men your age? If that

happened, you would endanger my life with the king!" Daniel then spoke to the warden whom the overseer of the court officials had appointed over Daniel, Hananiah, Mishael, and Azariah: "Please test your servants for ten days by providing us with some vegetables to eat and water to drink. Then compare our appearance with that of the young men who are eating the royal delicacies; deal with us in light of what you see." So the warden agreed to their proposal and tested them for ten days.

Daniel 1.9-14

Daniel had a big favor to ask. He would ask the overseer to put *his own life on the line for Daniel's convictions.* That's a lot of relational capital. In fact, the overseer explained just that. He let Daniel know in no uncertain terms that his life would be in jeopardy if he did what Daniel was asking.

Here is Daniel's moment of audacious faith. He went ahead and asked the overseer anyway. If his plan of testing them for ten days didn't work out, five lives would be lost. How many favors have you asked for that put five lives on the line? I can't think of one in my life, but that was the life of this tentmaker.

At the end of the ten days their appearance was better and their bodies were healthier than all the young men who had been eating the royal delicacies. So the warden removed the delicacies and the wine from their diet and gave them a diet of vegetables instead. Now as for these four young men, God endowed them with knowledge and skill in all sorts of literature and wisdom—and Daniel had insight into all kinds of visions and dreams.

When the time appointed by the king arrived, the overseer of the court officials brought them into Nebuchadnezzar's presence. When the king spoke with them, he did not find among the entire group anyone like Daniel, Hananiah, Mishael, or Azariah. So they entered the king's service. In every matter of wisdom and insight the king asked them about, he found them to be ten times better than any of the magicians and astrologers that were in his entire empire.

Daniel 1.15-20

And the result of this audacious faith? Daniel and his friends were healthier, stronger, smarter, and better looking than ever. Their answers were ten times better than their compatriots. It was a certain miracle, but we have every reason to believe that this miracle went on and on . . . for the next eighty years. If Daniel felt this conviction so powerfully as a youth, would he have simply let it go and compromised later on? Would he ever have defiled himself with these rich foods sacrificed to idols? Not at all. What we are witnessing in these few verses is a miracle of eighty years of more energy, more strength, more sharp wits than could be explained by caloric intake. This was the miracle of a lifetime because it lasted a lifetime.

There are no guarantees that God will work miraculously in your life as a tentmaker, but if he does, don't be surprised. You might find yourself in unexplained circumstances, and God might allow that blessing to go on and on and on.

There are no guarantees that God will work miraculously in your life as a tentmaker, but if he does, don't be surprised.

This whole scenario illustrates the wisdom of Proverbs 22.29:"Do you see a person skilled in his work? He will take his position before kings; he will not take his position before obscure people." What would it look like if you read that verse with yourself in it? "Are you skilled in your work? You will take your position before kings; you will not take your position before obscure people." In many places around the globe, tentmakers are a novelty because they are skilled expatriates. On account of this, they are often given a seat at the table, literally. One of my coworkers was invited into the king's palace to have tea with the king of Bahrain simply because she was there and he wanted to be hospitable to someone visiting his country.

DANIEL 2

Principle 10
Understand God's Ways with People

A S THE CREATOR OF ALL people, God relates to all people in wonderful ways. He understands the unique intricacies of each personality and what will speak to individuals, but he also knows what influences whole groups of people. Sometimes, we can draw patterns from how God touches the lives of those that he speaks to.

Across the Middle East and North Africa, dreams and visions have been instrumental in leading people to Jesus. This is something that Muslims bear witness to time and again when they profess faith in Christ. In fact, it is estimated that 90% of those who come to faith from a Muslim background see some sort of dream or vision that leads them to faith.

If Nebuchadnezzar is any indication, we can surmise that this is not only limited to Muslims, but more generally to the people of the Middle East even before the advent of Islam. Nebuchadnezzar was very sensitive to dreams, and he expected others to hold them in as high a regard as he did.

> In the second year of his reign Nebuchadnezzar had many dreams. His mind was disturbed and he suffered from insomnia. The king issued an order to summon the magicians, astrologers, sorcerers, and wise men in order to explain his dreams to him. So they came and awaited the king's instructions.
>
> The king told them, "I have had a dream, and I am anxious to understand the dream."
>
> *Daniel 2.1-3*

Nebuchadnezzar was suffering from insomnia or "dreaming dreams" as the original language says. These dreams disturbed him to such an extent that he disturbed others. Perhaps he figured, if he couldn't sleep, why should anyone else? So, he called in his wise men to explain his dreams to him, but since he was early in his reign, he had some suspicions about them and wondered if he was getting his money's worth, so to speak. Were these guys worth their salt? They were obviously living off of his dime, so he wanted to know if they really had insight into realms beyond the physical.

Nebuchadnezzar already had a couple of things going against him. Perhaps he was a bit unsure of himself since he was in his first few years as king. He may have had people trying to get rid of him before he consolidated a great deal of power. His father Nabonidus abandoned his kingdom for sixty years, leaving Nebuchadnezzar in charge, and it is uncertain whether Nabonidus ever returned from Arabia. Nebuchadnezzar may have been at risk of insurrection with the charge, "He's not the real king anyway," creating a bit of paranoia.

Second, he was dealing with long-term insomnia. If his insomnia had happened just one night, no one would have had a second thought and Daniel probably wouldn't have remembered it seventy years later. But this was a series of dreams that seemed to happen night after night for some time.

The wise men replied to the king: [What follows is in Aramaic] "O king, live forever! Tell your servants the dream, and we will disclose its interpretation." The king replied to the wise men, "My decision is firm. If you do not inform me of both the dream and its interpretation, you will be dismembered and your homes reduced to rubble! But if you can disclose the dream and its interpretation, you will receive from me gifts, a reward, and considerable honor. So disclose to me the dream and its interpretation!" They again replied, "Let the king inform us of the dream; then we will disclose its interpretation." The king replied, "I know for sure that you are attempting to gain time, because you see that my decision is firm. If you don't inform me of the dream, there is only one thing that is going to happen to you. For you have agreed among yourselves to report to me something false and deceitful until such time as things might change. So tell me the dream, and I will have confidence that you can disclose its interpretation."

The wise men replied to the king, "There is no man on earth who is able to disclose the king's secret, for no king, regardless of his position and power, has ever requested such a thing from any magician, astrologer, or wise man. What the king is asking is too difficult, and no one exists who can disclose it to the king, except for the gods—but they don't live among mortals!"

Daniel 2.4-11

Insomnia is a real threat to a person's capacity to rationally process normal events. I experienced this personally when insomnia over months of time made me susceptible to irrational thoughts and fears as a tentmaker. Nebuchadnezzar could certainly relate to those feelings and that may be why we read of his irrational request of his sorcerers and magicians. Not only did he want them to interpret his dream, but he wanted them to tell him his dream. Of course, he would recognize right away if they were accurate in the dream's story or if they were just pulling his leg. This was unheard of because it really is far beyond any human explanation. If the gods really did speak to these magicians, sorcerers, and wise men, Nebuchadnezzar would know it. If not, this witch trial would cleanse the palace of this charade once and for all. If they couldn't tell him his dream and interpret it, they were worthless to him. The subsequent conclusion to this is that if the gods (or God) really did come through and tell him this superhuman information, he was spiritually open to its message in his life.

This is the case again across the Middle East and North Africa where people are seeking spiritual messages from God, especially during the month of Ramadan, the month of Muslim fasting. Their spiritual sensitivities are heightened, and they are more aware and open to messages from God. Many Muslims pray to receive messages during this month and even more so on the Night of Power when their prophet Muhammed is said to have received a vision that he was transported into heaven. They are looking to heaven for messages leading them to the truth in the same way that Nebuchadnezzar did, and they are more ready to apprehend those messages and the impact on their lives during this month.

As a tentmaker, pray for the Lord to powerfully use this natural openness. The dynamic power of a dream given to one or to many people during this month can sway the thinking of whole families to the truth of the Gospel.

Recognize, too, that God speaks differently to different people groups. It is estimated that 90% of Hindus who come to faith in Jesus experience some sort of physical manifestation of God's power like a healing or a physical sign or wonder. Most Westerners are moved by rational, logical reasoning because it "makes sense." The point is that God understands hearts and often moves in similar manner to soften the hearts of those who have not heard.

As an example of this, one of my friends, Abdullah, who came to faith in Christ from Islam, told me that he saw visions or dreams of Jesus leading him away from Islam five or six times before he finally came to faith in Jesus. I just about choked when I heard him say he saw five or six manifestations of Jesus! How many does it take?? You would think one would be enough, but five or six times before it sinks in? Then again, I know the hardness of my own heart. If the Lord had used dreams and visions to speak to me, it probably would have taken more than five or six dreams and visions.

So, pray for powerful dreams and visions and signs and wonders and healings in your tentmaking and be prepared to walk people through the truth to which they might be exposed.

Principle 11
Be Winsome to Win Some

Because of this the king got furiously angry and gave orders to destroy all the wise men of Babylon. So a decree went out, and the wise men were about to be executed. They also sought Daniel and his friends so that they could be executed.

Then Daniel spoke with prudent counsel to Arioch, who was in charge of the king's executioners and who had gone out to execute the wise men of Babylon. He inquired of Arioch the king's deputy, "Why is the decree from the king so urgent?" Then Arioch informed Daniel about the matter. So Daniel went in and requested the king to grant him time, that he might disclose the interpretation to the king.

Daniel 2.12-16

Daniel not only gained rapport with Ashpenaz in chapter one, but he earned relational capital with Arioch and even with the king. We can see this through the king's response to Daniel's request. When the other wise men explained that coming to know and interpret the dream was too difficult, he accused them of stalling and ordered that they be killed. When Daniel asked for more time, the king was sympathetic and granted the request.

Daniel was a winsome guy. He was a likable sort of person, and we can see that from his friendships throughout these chapters. We don't have descriptions of him as a friend, but we see the effects of his winsome personality through his reception by a number of people. He didn't have a lot of rough edges, and he didn't make it difficult to be around him.

Think for a minute of how stark a contrast this is to other very successful, powerful people today. Take, for example, Steve Jobs. Steve Jobs was a brilliant man with an uncanny knack for innovation and marketing. That being said, he was a difficult person to be around. Even his closest business partners could barely stand working with him. [16]

With Daniel, we simply don't get that impression. Instead, we get the indication of quiet humility from an intelligent man who was (*gasp*) fun to be around. Even the king was willing to delay his unbreakable edict. He was willing to delay the execution of the wise men at the mere request of Daniel. What a lesson for us!

Our aim as believers is to fulfill the Great Commission by sharing the reason for the hope within us and we do this with all courtesy and respect in good conscience (1 Peter 3.15). We want to win souls for Christ. Daniel models this by being winsome to win some.

Principle 12
Initiate a Massive Movement of Prayer

> Then Daniel went to his home and informed his friends Hananiah, Mishael, and Azariah of the matter. He asked them to pray for mercy from the God of heaven concerning this mystery so that he and his friends would not be destroyed along with the rest of the wise men of Babylon.
>
> *Daniel 2.17-18*

This note is so short and pithy, it almost seems like an afterthought. "Would you pray for mercy from the God of heaven? Oh, and pick up a gallon of milk from the grocery store, too." Yet it is one of the linchpin verses that holds together the entire book. "Pray for mercy from the God of heaven." If Daniel would not have received mercy from the God of heaven, we never would have known about Daniel. He wouldn't have survived until his later years, and he wouldn't have written this book to recount the amazing things God did. We wouldn't have known about the amazing sustenance of his vegetable and water diet. We wouldn't have known about the fiery furnace. We wouldn't have known about the handwriting on the wall. We wouldn't have the Sunday School story about Daniel and the lion's den. And we wouldn't have some of the most accurate prophecies ever recorded which come later in the book. Again, God came through in a very supernatural way with mercy from the God of heaven.

As important as this is that God came through, it happened because of prayer. We learn from this that prayer is essential to the whole book of Daniel and all of the stories we know from it. Prayer is the linchpin.

Maybe Daniel's three friends don't qualify as an army of prayer warriors. Whether it is three or an army, we know the power of prayer in Daniel's life. Why wouldn't we amass all the prayer we can in our lives? When you go out as a tentmaker, enlist an army of people to pray for you. Don't be picky and choosy about who should be praying for you. Begin a massive movement of prayer for the people you are working with and, more directly, for you as you work among them. Here are a few ideas for practically applying Daniel's example:

1. Educate your prayer partners. They are looking to you as their expert on this people group. Take advantage of that position as their expert to share with them information they won't find on the Internet.

2. Share specific people or instances or places that you pray for, but do it judiciously. I rarely advise sharing personally identifying information about the people you are working with, but you can still build a persona in the minds of your prayer partners with the specifics you are praying for. For example, you might have Fatima in mind, but you could ask your prayer partners to pray for F. that she would get past her resistance to the authority of the Bible.

3. Include people in your prayer walks or prayer drives through description. Tell people when you will be going on a prayer walk or prayer drive through parts of your city, and ask them to pray with you at that time. Share with them what you learned or what stood out to you about the needs of the city. Explain how you are praying against the forces of the local temple, for example, and enjoin people to pray with you.

4. Share resources that your prayer partners can turn to in order to engage more through informed prayer. The book *Operation World* is an excellent, thorough resource. Prayercast.com has attractive video prayers for every country on the planet. Joshuaproject.net has detailed information on every people group around the globe.

5. Use technology, but use it wisely. As much of a blessing as it may be to fire off prayer requests to 200 people, recognize that there are then 200 digital copies of the prayer requests you just wrote.

6. There is great responsibility in sharing prayer requests. Never share anything you wouldn't want to be widely known.

7. A final lesson to point out from Daniel's example is that he drew back for a personal retreat when he needed to hear from the Lord. You would think he had more pressing matters to tend to rather than "taking a day off" for prayer. Couldn't he spend his time better by strategizing with the think tank he was a part of? Couldn't they find some way out of this bind through legal measures to find the king unreasonable and incompetent for office? Surely, there were better things that Daniel could have done rather than head home for a "mini-vacation." Let me put it this way, taking time away for prayer is the least we can do, and it's the most we can do.

Taking time away for prayer is the least we can do, and it's the most we can do.

Principle 13
Respond in Faith

Then in a night vision the mystery was revealed to Daniel. So Daniel praised the God of heaven, saying,

"Let the name of God be praised forever and ever,
for wisdom and power belong to him.
He changes times and seasons,
deposing some kings
and establishing others.
He gives wisdom to the wise;
he imparts knowledge to those with understanding;
he reveals deep and hidden things.

He knows what is in the darkness,
and light resides with him.

O God of my fathers, I acknowledge and glorify you,
for you have bestowed wisdom and power on me.
Now you have enabled me to understand what I requested from you.
For you have enabled me to understand the
king's dilemma."

Daniel 2.19-23

Even in the face of certain death if he was wrong, Daniel gives a striking example of unrivaled faith. His response once he sees the night vision of Nebuchadnezzar's
dream is absolute confidence that God has answered his
prayers. He didn't wait until he got confirmation from
Nebuchadnezzar that he saw the right dream, rather, he
immediately responded in praise to the only God who
could deliver in such a time of need. God's superiority
over the inadequacies of the Babylonian gods was un-
mistakable, and Daniel knew it.

With this example in mind, take courage in your hour
of need. When you call out to the Lord with your requests and the Lord delivers, be ready with immediate
faith, giving all the glory to him alone. Take comfort
from Jesus' encouragement knowing that "your Father
knows what you need before you ask him" (Matthew
6.8). He is with you always.

In the midst of this amazing testimony of God's greatness and superiority over all kings, is it boastful of Daniel to just happen to mention that "God bestowed wisdom and power on [him]"? Again, I will say that, no,
recognizing the gifts that God had given Daniel was not
boastful, but rather, humble as a simple description of

reality. In the very next phrase he attributes the honor to the Lord who gave him this wisdom and granted him the answer to his prayer. He's not claiming accolades for himself that his ingenuity entitles him to. He is clearly honoring God by describing the Lord's gracious gifts, even though those gifts happen to be qualities intrinsic to Daniel's person.

So, when the Lord grants you the request you've been asking for, don't take credit as though it is something you have done. Honor God even with the great things he gives to you as gifts.

Daniel adeptly explains exactly this in verse 30 with the words, "As for me, this mystery was revealed to me not because I possess more wisdom than any other living person. . . ." Daniel made clear that this amazing ability was only a gift.

When you do great work as a tentmaker, give credit to whom credit is due. This applies to coworkers and colleagues that you may need to highlight at the completion of an important project, but even more importantly, recognize that these opportunities themselves are an opportunity for you to confess the gifts and abilities the Lord has built into you. You might be called in to be congratulated in front of the CEO and the board of directors of your organization. Think of the power of an apt word, saying, "God has given me gifts and abilities for all the work I do, and I'm the person I am only because of the change that Jesus made in my life." This would not be offensive or unlawful anywhere in the world. Think through what you will say in advance because as we already noted, a person skilled in his work "will take his position before kings; he will not take his position before obscure people" (Proverbs 22.29).

Daniel 3

Principle 14
You Can't Clean a Fish before You Catch It

My wife learned this great principle in her high school youth group that she has shared with me many times. I might express some frustration at the depravity of the world and the way that our society is on an uninterrupted crash course into immorality, and she will calmly respond, "You can't clean a fish before you catch it." Maybe it's her calm, unruffled resolve that so strongly puts me in my place, but I have to admit, she's right.

Jesus has made us fishers of people, and we can't expect those people to act like faithful followers of Jesus before they've experienced the love of Jesus. We can't expect them to live the moral lives of believers when they are not believers. Instead, they will continue in their immorality until the Lord opens their blind eyes to see another way, the way of Jesus. Without the Lord's intervention to make blind eyes see, we can't expect a blind person to see. It certainly doesn't help to shout louder that they should be able to see. They're blind.

King Nebuchadnezzar had a golden statue made. It was 90 feet tall and nine feet wide. He erected it on the plain of Dura in the province of Babylon.

Then King Nebuchadnezzar sent out a summons to assemble the satraps, prefects, governors, counselors, treasurers, judges, magistrates, and all the other authorities of the province to attend the dedication of the statue that he had erected. So the satraps, prefects, governors, counselors, treasurers, judges, magistrates, and all the other provincial authorities assembled for the dedication of the statue that King Nebuchadnezzar had erected. They were standing in front of the statue that Nebuchadnezzar had erected.

Daniel 3.1-3

This chapter in the book of Daniel launches right into the building of a massive statue of Nebuchadnezzar, who intended all the people of the land to worship it. Even though Nebuchadnezzar had just expressed his conclusion in Daniel chapter 2 that Daniel's God was "a God of Gods and Lord of kings," this profession of superiority obviously was not a profession of faith in that very same God. He was not a believer. Yet. And he didn't act like a believer. Yet.

Obviously, Daniel and his friends would have opposed the building of this statue, and they certainly would have advised against it. In this story, though, the actors have changed, and it isn't explained exactly where Daniel was. Some have conjectured that he was sick at the time, and others think that he was sent away on official business. No matter the reason, Daniel is not in this story and his three friends take center stage in their steps of faith. By the way, by this point they were now only called by their Babylonian names, Shadrach, Meshach and Abednego.

Now at that time certain Chaldeans came forward and brought malicious accusations against the Jews. They said to King Nebuchadnezzar, "O king, live forever! You have issued an edict, O king, that everyone must bow down and pay homage to the golden statue when they hear the sound of the horn, flute, zither, trigon, harp, pipes, and all kinds of music. And whoever does not bow down and pay homage must be thrown into the midst of a furnace of blazing fire. But there are Jewish men whom you appointed over the administration of the province of Babylon—Shadrach, Meshach, and Abednego—and these men have not shown proper respect to you, O king. They don't serve your gods and they don't pay homage to the golden statue that you have erected."

Daniel 3.8-12

Much to the chagrin of Shadrach, Meshach, and Abednego, Nebuchadnezzar is adamant in his insistence that people worship his statue. His mind is fixed, at least for now. Even though he's shown progress with steps toward what we would think of as faith, he is still a fish in the sea that has not been caught.

When I lived as a tentmaker in the Middle East, I cannot tell you how many times I saw people take steps toward faith where they clearly spoke against the predominant belief system and affirmed the beliefs of the Christian faith. As delighted as I was when these people made these statements and seemed to respond to discussions about faith, my heart plummeted as much into real grief when I realized that they had not fully embraced faith in Jesus. My emotions were on a roller coaster of elation and despair for these friends that I loved. Day by day I would either be up or I would be down—sometimes making a full swing in the same day—with the comments of my friends.

This roller coaster showed me very clearly that the faith of my friends would not be on account of my crafty apologetics arguments or logical reasoning. Yes, the Lord might use those discussions to remove stumbling blocks, but their faith or lack of faith was entirely a move of the Spirit on their hearts. I would not reason them from death to life.

My response could have been disillusionment. Others in the circle of Christian missions have given up on evangelizing (i.e. sharing the Good News with) Muslims. Obviously, that would have been walking in the direction away from fulfilling the Great Commission. Instead, this roller coaster drew me closer to the Lord in prayer for my friends because I recognized clearly that God had to remove the blindness from their eyes. Rather than driving me away from sharing the truth, it refocused my sharing of the truth and strengthened my dependence on the Savior.

Don't be discouraged if you find yourself on this roller coaster. It was familiar to those proclaiming the truth to Nebuchadnezzar as well, and his story continued its path to faith in God as we will see.

Principle 15
You Will Encounter Slanderous Opposition
Look again at this passage.

Now at that time certain Chaldeans came forward and brought malicious accusations against the Jews. They said to King Nebuchadnezzar, "O king, live forever! You have issued an edict, O king, that everyone must bow down and pay homage to the golden statue when they hear the sound of the horn, flute, zither, trigon, harp, pipes, and all kinds of music. And whoever does not bow down and pay homage must be thrown into the midst of a furnace of blazing fire. But there are Jewish men whom you appointed over the administration of the province of Babylon—Shadrach, Meshach, and Abednego— and these men have not shown proper respect to you, O king. They don't serve your gods and they don't pay homage to the golden statue that you have erected."

Daniel 3.8-12

Note the destructive power of slander and, subsequently, malicious gossip. After all, malicious gossip is simply anonymous slander.

What is at the root of this destructive force in human relationships? At risk of answering a question with a question, what do you observe about the people that slandered Shadrach, Meshach and Abednego?

One of the first things we can understand from chapter 1 is that they were trained along with Shadrach, Meshach and Abednego. We know that because they were Chaldeans who worked their way to having an audience with the king. The slanderers had similar training, similar skills, better food, and yet they couldn't hold a candle to Shadrach, Meshach and Abednego in their God-given abilities. This led to certain jealousy. You name the benefit, Shadrach, Meshach and Abednego had it, and these Chaldeans did not.

When these three were made administrators over the whole province of Babylon, the others became not just jealous of the abilities but of the position and favor that these men enjoyed. Not only did Shadrach, Meshach, and Abednego have the God-given abilities, but they gained position, authority, and even proximity to the king.

Though jealousy may not be the root of all slander, it is definitely one of the most common. Of course, there are other roots of slander, like hatred and psychopathic intent to destroy, but jealousy is likely the most common.

The next questions might be, "What's the harm in a little slander? Who can't tolerate a few evil words spoken against them? Who can't tolerate a few fiery arrows shot from a cloak of anonymity?"

Let the original Aramaic text explain this itself. When we read verse 8 in English, we read the rather tame translation, "Now at that time certain Chaldeans came forward and brought malicious accusations against the Jews." The Aramaic is a bit more forthcoming and would be translated literally, "Now at that time certain Chaldeans came forward and ate the pieces of the Jews."[17]

This is the net effect of slander and gossip. It will not be fair. It will not follow any set of rules, whether in your culture or in your host culture. As a tentmaker who is faithfully working as to the Lord and not to men, you will be undermined by others' attempts to destroy you. Whatever the form of the attack, jealousy or something worse is at its root.

Malicious slander and gossip do not have to be carried out through something as public as an editorial in a newspaper or a billboard on the street, although today's social media certainly approximates that capability for everyone. Instead, verse 10 shows the much more common approach of malicious intent being exercised through official means. For example, reporting a workplace infraction is justified, and even in Daniel 3 these accusers had the right to do that. However, it was evident to Daniel and any reader of this account, that these accusers were watching for some way to bring these godly men down. They were carefully pursuing Daniel's friends like a predator pursues its prey, watching for any mistake, even a small one, that would give them the advantage and allow them to take down Shadrach, Meshach, and Abednego. This difference between reporting an infraction for correction and pursuing someone for destruction is easily recognizable.

After the Chaldeans brought their complaints, the matter could have been dropped for lack of merit, but Nebuchadnezzar did not put an end to the slander. Then again, he was not the best example of leadership. Rather, the leadership entertained the slander and acted on it. He gave it a voice. Even today, this is the easier response, though it is not the countercultural, courageous response Jesus calls leadership to. Jesus calls us to a higher standard as individuals and certainly as leaders:

> If your brother sins, go and show him his fault when the two of you are alone. If he listens to you, you have regained your brother. But if he does not listen, take one or two others with you, so that at the testimony of two or three witnesses every matter may be established. If he refuses to listen to them, tell it to the church. If he refuses to listen to the church, treat him like a Gentile or a tax collector.
> *Matthew 18.15-17*

After the very first step of Jesus' model of approaching your brother privately, leadership is involved. Yet, as a tentmaker, you cannot assume that you will be treated respectfully by your coworkers and you cannot assume that the leadership you work under will respond in a godly manner. Leadership might entertain slander or gossip which might undermine your ability to work. Nonetheless, it is not for you to begrudge their response, but rather, to continue faithfully in your work "as to the Lord and not to men."

In one job I had, there was person who had a problem with me where he thought I had dropped the ball and I thought he had dropped the ball. I knew he was upset, so I approached him privately. As it happened, this person dug in his heels, left the room, and went to my boss.

My boss, as a believer in a Christian organization, stopped this other person short and said, "It sounds like David already reached out to you to deal with this. If you have a problem with David, you need to take it up with David. I don't need to get involved." That sort of response modeled what Jesus taught in Matthew 18. Stepping out of that model and doing things our own way is like pouring gas on a fire. If we aren't careful, those flames might just consume us.

DANIEL 4

Principle 16
Beware of Syncretism

"King Nebuchadnezzar, to all peoples, nations, and language groups that live in all the land: Peace and prosperity! I am delighted to tell you about the signs and wonders that the most high God has done for me.

"How great are his signs!
How mighty are his wonders!
His kingdom will last forever,
and his authority continues from one generation
to the next."

Daniel 4.1-3

Nebuchadnezzar now gives a third profession of the superiority of the Most High God in the verses above, but in reality, he is simply adding this to his collection of gods to worship and he still names Bel as his god later in this chapter. This is the practice of syncretism, that is, combining different religious beliefs. Nebuchadnezzar still believes Bel is his god, but he adds worship of Daniel's God.

Although it is your desire to see people in your host country know Jesus, it is very important not to put words into their mouths or assume more than they say about their faith themselves. For us, from our American culture with its roots in monotheism, we see following God as an either/or. By their nature, monotheistic religions are exclusivist. Either you have faith in God as it is described in the religion, or you don't. In Daniel's case, either you believed the Torah, the history books, and the wisdom literature, or you didn't. The same is the case for Christians ministering to Muslims today. Either people believe what the Bible says about God, or they believe what the Qur'an says about God. There is no room for combining the two and worshiping both. They are absolutely exclusivist.

For a polytheist, on the other hand, it is no problem to add worship of another god. Just as Nebuchadnezzar tacked on the worship of "the most high God," modern-day Hindus do the same. When we present Jesus as the Son of God, Hindus add that belief to their collection and worship Jesus as a manifestation of Krishna. For you, when working as a tentmaker, this discernment of syncretism is always something to be aware of and to be ready to counter. Perhaps the most well-known claim of absolute authority is in Jesus' words himself. Here, he includes an additional denial of there being any other way to God:

Jesus replied, "I am the way, and the truth, and the life. No one comes to the Father except through me."
John 14.6

Not only is this an exclusive claim about being the only way to God, but it is an explicit denial of any other way to God. It's positive and negative. There simply is no room for the most high God to be added into the worship of other gods.

Principle 17
Sanctification Is a Process

> "This is the dream that I, King Nebuchadnezzar, saw. Now you, Belteshazzar, declare its interpretation, for none of the wise men in my kingdom are able to make known to me the interpretation. But you can do so, for a spirit of the holy gods is in you."
>
> *Daniel 4.18*

We've seen throughout the book of Daniel and we see again in verse 18 that none of the other wise men were worth their salt. When the time came that they were really needed, they had nothing to offer. When they were not needed, they had plenty of advice!

Even so, Nebuchadnezzar kept seeking their advice. He recognized the superior spirit in Daniel, but the king kept turning to the familiar ways of his people and culture.

Tentmakers, too, will find that people turn to their own people and their own ways even after they've seen that the advice of their people has been shown to be worthless. Host people might turn to medicinal cures that are more closely aligned with shamanism rather than science or biblical faith. If these people have not made a profession of faith, it is important to remind yourself, you can't clean a fish before you catch it. If this person has made a profession of faith, patiently teach, reprove, correct, and train in righteousness and understand that no one is sanctified in an instant. It seems that

Western Christians expect new non-Western Christians to immediately recognize all of the practices of the "old man" in their lives and abandon them without instruction. Yet, all new Christians need to be instructed from Scripture as to what the right way is. If you see someone abandon their sinful ways immediately, the person was almost certainly raised as a cultural "Christian" with years of training through Sunday School or church attendance or parental guidance or the faithful prayers of grandparents. In other words, God has been preparing them for the sanctification process for years before they make a profession of faith. When working with the unreached, it is important to recognize that you are laying the groundwork for the first time. You are establishing the foundation, so it is wise to be patient and continually direct these new believers to Scripture so that they, too, can be educated well in discerning good from evil.

So, yes, you should point out when a new believer drifts into their old ways, but do this in an understanding way, knowing that they may have lived a life that was blind to the truth. They may never have seen the truth, and they need a caring friend to gently point them in the right way.

Principle 18
The Most High God Is King of Kings and Lord of Lords

Nebuchadnezzar had another nightmare. It was terrifying, and again, he asked his astrologers and magicians to interpret the dream, but they were of no help. Then, he turned to his good friend Daniel who was much better at interpreting dreams. Nebuchadnezzar was awaiting its interpretation on pins and needles.

Then Daniel (whose name is also Belteshazzar) was upset for a brief time; his thoughts were alarming him. The king said, "Belteshazzar, don't let the dream and its interpretation alarm you." But Belteshazzar replied, "Sir, if only the dream were for your enemies and its interpretation applied to your adversaries! The tree that you saw that grew large and strong, whose top reached to the sky, and which could be seen in all the land, whose foliage was attractive and its fruit plentiful, and from which there was food available for all, under whose branches wild animals used to live, and in whose branches birds of the sky used to nest— it is you, O king! For you have become great and strong. Your greatness is such that it reaches to heaven, and your authority to the ends of the earth. As for the king seeing a holy sentinel coming down from heaven and saying, 'Chop down the tree and destroy it, but leave its taproot in the ground, with a band of iron and bronze around it, surrounded by the grass of the field. Let it become damp with the dew of the sky, and let it live with the wild animals, until seven periods of time go by for him'— this is the interpretation, O king! It is the decision of the Most High that this has happened to my lord the king. You will be driven from human society, and you will live with the wild animals. You will be fed grass like oxen, and you will become damp with the dew of the sky. Seven periods of time will pass by for you, before you understand that the Most High is ruler over human kingdoms and gives them to whomever he wishes. They said to leave the taproot of the tree, for your kingdom will be restored to you when you come to understand that heaven rules. Therefore, O king, may my advice be pleasing to you. Break away from your sins by doing what is right, and from your iniquities by showing mercy to the poor. Perhaps your prosperity will be prolonged."

Daniel 4.19-27

Daniel was troubled in verse 19 by what he saw as the interpretation of the dream for Nebuchadnezzar, and it was obvious to the king that Daniel was a bit unsettled about telling him what he really saw.

Think of it, Daniel was in a tricky place. If he told the king, "Well, Mr. King, you're going to get the axe," Daniel might have gotten the axe. On the other hand, if he watered down the message or didn't tell what he saw, not only would it be a violation of conscience for Daniel, but he might have gotten the axe! We've already seen with the dream in Daniel 2 that Nebuchadnezzar didn't tolerate "yes men" who were faithless and just told him what he wanted to hear. By all appearances, Daniel is in a lose-lose situation.

The situation Nebuchadnezzar is in isn't much better. He's going to get the axe. Herod was in a similar state much later in Acts 12 when he gave a particularly rousing TED Talk.[18] The crowds responded by crying out, "The voice of a god, and not of a man!" Herod rather enjoyed this when he should have been denouncing it. The result? He was infested by flesh-eating worms and died.

Nebuchadnezzar suffered from the same complex of believing himself to be in the place of God. In some ways, a death like Herod's might have been easier than the insanity that Nebuchadnezzar received, but the point is that every ruler, no matter how powerful, is under the sovereign authority of the most high God. The sentence of Herod or the sentence of Nebuchadnezzar could be-fall any world leader then or now. It's almost unthink-able, but could you imagine the President of the United States being driven out of the White House by the Spirit of God to mow the National Mall with his teeth? His upcoming re-election bid might be a bit stunted.

We tend to confine the power of God to biblical times, but it is the same God at work in our world today. The same sentence could be handed down to the Prime Min-ister of the United Kingdom or the King of Saudi Arabia. It is still the same sovereign God who reigns over the world, and it is still the same, frail humanity that is sub-servient to him.

For the tentmaker, this is an encouragement. If God can forcibly depose the most powerful, he can forcibly act on the less prestigious. As verse 27 says, even the most powerful can be "weighed on the balances and found to be lacking." If God can handle such major king-doms in such dramatic fashion, he can certainly manage our people problems.

Most biblical studies students have never been kicked out of a pastoral counseling class, but I have. Here, I was in the first semester of my senior year and I had gained a re-spect for the counseling approach called Nouthetic Coun-seling, but my instructor did not share my view. In the last week of the course, he referred to Nouthetic Counseling repeatedly as he underscored his view of the shortcomings of the approach, and it seemed to me that he was looking at me and directing his comments right to me.

I didn't want to start an issue, so I simply kept my head down and didn't make eye contact with him. After some minutes, my professor stopped his lecture and said, "Da-vid, would you please leave?" I didn't ask any questions and simply left. It wasn't the happiest day for either of us, but he later explained that it just looked like I was very frustrated. He cared so much about me that he didn't want to make me sit through class frustrated, and he decided he would talk to me later.

In spite of it all, this professor became one of my trusted counselors and advisors over the next years, even after I left college. Not only that, he became one of my financial supporters when I served overseas for many years. God can move hearts even when we are stubborn. To this day we are still personal friends. You see, our people-problems are not so great as we often make them out to be. God can move major kingdoms and he can even move my own stubborn heart. I somehow think the latter is more difficult.

DANIEL 5

IT WAS AN EXTREME PARTY. One thousand VIPs. Alcohol flowing like a river. Sex slaves. Strippers. This wasn't folly of youth. This was debauchery.

In the midst of this, the host had the brilliant idea of pulling out some pure gold and silver chalices to drink from. Why not, right? Those Jews in Israel certainly weren't using them as they sat in storage in Babylon. This guy wanted to throw a party no one would ever forget.

King Belshazzar prepared a great banquet for a thousand of his nobles, and he was drinking wine in front of them all. While under the influence of the wine, Belshazzar issued an order to bring in the gold and silver vessels—the ones that Nebuchadnezzar his father had confiscated from the temple in Jerusalem—so that the king and his nobles, together with his wives and his concubines, could drink from them. So they brought the gold and silver vessels that had been confiscated from the temple, the house of God in Jerusalem, and the king and his nobles, together with his wives and concubines, drank from them. As they drank wine, they praised the gods of gold and silver, bronze, iron, wood, and stone.

Daniel 5.1-4

Everything was going along just fine from their point of view until God showed up. In a scene that could only be imagined in a Halloween horror flick, the fingers of a human hand crawled along the wall in front of the host of the party and began carving a message into the plaster. Undoubtedly, some party goers screamed in terror, feeling all their worst nightmares were coming alive in front of them. Some probably thought this was a party trick by the king's magicians. Some probably thought they were hallucinating and their minds were playing tricks on them because of the alcohol, but everyone else was "hallucinating" the same thing—ain't no hallucination.

At that very moment the fingers of a human hand appeared and wrote on the plaster of the royal palace wall, opposite the lampstand. The king was watching the back of the hand that was writing. Then all the color drained from the king's face and he became alarmed. The joints of his hips gave way, and his knees began knocking together. The king called out loudly to summon the astrologers, wise men, and diviners. The king proclaimed to the wise men of Babylon that anyone who could read this inscription and disclose its interpretation would be clothed in purple and have a golden collar placed on his neck and be third ruler in the kingdom.

Daniel 5.5-7

An inevitable stampede for the doors was stopped by people realizing it was an actual message going into the plaster of the wall. It looked like a dead man's hand, but, come on, no human hand could claw through hardened plaster and stone! Letter by letter brought a pall of silence to the room with the exception of the sound of broken pieces of the wall falling to the floor.

The host, who happened to be the young king Belshazzar, was paralyzed in fear, watching the terrifying scene unfold, but he likely did not stay put by choice. His knees knocked in terror and even the joints of his hips gave way, preventing any escape. Once the carving of his palace stopped, he screamed for someone to bring his answer-people to tell him what was going on. The wise men, astrologers, and spiritual diviners were brought forward, but in the end, they admitted, "Dude, no idea. We got nothing."

Name your horror film, but this one matched them all in real life, and it started with the Great Gatsby-style party scene where most faithful followers of Jesus would not go.

Principle 19
In the World but Not of the World

Tentmakers intentionally go to people in these places. Weird, huh? They're not rebelling against God or satisfying some prurient desire by hanging around these people. It's just that sinners are the ones who need Jesus, so tentmakers go right at it and live among them. The fact is, these sinners don't know that they should live any other way. That's why they need tentmakers.

So, tentmakers live among people who have different moral standards. Those people might be drunk at times as was clearly described here with Belshazzar and his entourage. They might be carousing at parties with sex slaves which is what a *concubine* was. They might be watching strippers, which was, apparently, a pastime of Babylonian kings. It's recorded in Esther 1.11, for example, that King Ahasuerus commanded Queen Vashti, to come "show the people and the officials her beauty" and that *showing* carries a sense of sensuality and impropriety for a king to ask his queen to show to anyone else. It's likely this was happening at Belshazzar's party, and it's likely that you will encounter pornography, incest, sexual abuse, sex slavery, polygamy, and other sexual sins happening around you as a tentmaker.

Many of these activities repulse us by their very nature, but others are subtle lures that can ensnare people who haven't given forethought to their moral limits. For example, seeing pornography openly displayed on a newstand in France is commonplace, so what will you do to guard your mind when you are legitimately looking for a copy of *The Economist*? Perhaps it means sending your wife to buy *The Economist*, or perhaps it means you have the magazine shipped to your home to avoid the temptation altogether.

The tentmaker has to consider in advance what to participate in, what to avoid, and what to strongly protest. Ideally, this refusal would not unnecessarily offend the hosts while necessarily allowing the truth of Jesus to offend where necessary.

For example, *qat* is a mild hallucinogenic drug that is chewed recreationally and socially in the southern Arabian peninsula. To refuse it when a host offers it is an insult, but knowing some cultural clues in advance can help you avoid the moral compromise of getting intoxicated by this drug. The tip is to simply put it in your mouth once, then spit it out before experiencing its hallucinogenic effects. This gives you an excuse for not partaking ever again because it is socially acceptable to say, "I've tried it, and I just don't care for it." This will not offend the host whereas outright refusal will offend.

Even so, there may be a time when you need to confront a friend who uses *qat* every day along with everyone else and his mind is wasted every afternoon and evening. There may come an opportunity to challenge him, saying, "What is your purpose in life? You chew *qat* every day and you can't think straight about what life is all about. When are you going to consider what has real meaning in life?"

This sort of approach—avoiding needless offense while letting truth bear its offense—will make you a person of impact among the people you serve.

In your massive reading and study about the people among whom you will be living (see Principle 7), think through the issues that you learn about these people that might be a compromise. Think through how you will answer them while maintaining your integrity and not compromising your moral position.

This sort of approach—avoiding needless offense while letting truth bear its offense—will make you a person of impact among the people you serve. Daniel was sought out even decades after his prime because of the powerful Spirit of the Lord that worked in him.

There is a man in your kingdom who has within him a spirit of the holy gods. In the days of your father, he proved to have insight, discernment, and wisdom like that of the gods. King Nebuchadnezzar your father appointed him chief of the magicians, astrologers, wise men, and diviners. Thus there was found in this man Daniel, whom the king renamed Belteshazzar, an extraordinary spirit, knowledge, and skill to interpret dreams, solve riddles, and decipher knotty problems. Now summon Daniel, and he will disclose the interpretation."

Daniel 5.11-12

This is a powerful testimony to the faithfulness of Daniel and the value that he was to the Babylonian leadership. There are two points that can be drawn from this. First, what a legacy! Again, we see how the value of the wisdom and insights Daniel gave were so highly regarded that he was thought of decades after his prime and certainly well into his "retirement." We don't get the idea that he was still actively leading in the kingdom, but this old man who had peaked long ago was the person that was sought after for the king's imminent need.

What if Daniel had thrown some adult temper tantrum when he was removed from office?

Where in Daniel 5 do we read the names of any other advisors to the king? Did their advice and reputation last? Not at all. Their advice drifted away long earlier. How about Ashpenaz or Arioch who were named earlier in the book? Do we read anything about them even though they were superiors to Daniel? No, their memory and influence had passed away as well. Even though Daniel was "inferior" in his position to these men, his influence carried on much longer. The last had become first, and the first had become last.

The second point from this passage is the question, what if Daniel had given up? What if he had really retired from service and didn't bother to keep his mind sharp or engaged because he was no longer needed? What if Daniel had thrown some adult temper tantrum when he was removed from office and refused to be available to the king? We don't get that impression from this great man. With a commendable measure of grace, he makes his management consultant services available to the king *pro bono*. This man was honorable to the extreme.

As believers in Jesus, we are in the world. We can't do anything about that. But, we are not of the world. Part of God's commission to us is to model righteousness and justice even in the face of the world's depravity. In this, tentmakers are on the front lines.

Principle 20
Preach the Gospel at All Times

Saint Francis of Assisi is often quoted (or misquoted as the case actually is) as having said, "Preach the Gospel at all times. When necessary use words." Someone could get the impression that this is what is meant by tentmaking, that tentmakers really only witness passively through their lifestyle and actions without having to go through the challenge of thinking through appropriate words to share the Good News with people.

We might think that because of Daniel's powerful testimony and work ethic, people simply "knew" that he was a follower of God and this didn't need explanation by words.

Let's interact with that a bit.

Did Daniel rely on just his actions? Not at all. If that were the case, one would expect this chapter to be a shining example of not needing words, given Belshazzar's effusive commendation of Daniel.

> I have heard about you, how there is a spirit of the gods in you, and how you have insight, discernment, and extraordinary wisdom.
>
> *Daniel 5.14*

Instead, when Daniel has the opportunity to recount *A Modern History of Iraq through the 540s B.C.* for Belshazzar's benefit, here is what Daniel actually testifies to:

- God gave Belshazzar's father, Nebuchadnezzar, the kingdom (verse 18). We know from chapter 4 that God did this twice.
- God bestowed on Nebuchadnezzar fear before all nations (verse 19).
- God rules over human kingdoms (verse 21).
- Belshazzar exalted himself against God (verse 23).
- Belshazzar has not glorified God (verse 23).
- God controls even Belshazzar's breath and all of his ways (verse 23).
- God sent the hand on the wall (verse 24).
- God has determined the length of Belshazzar's kingdom (verse 26).

So, Daniel took Belshazzar to school on the greatness of God. He did not shrink back, and he sure didn't let his actions speak for themselves. He spoke the truth. He took every opportunity to share the truth about God even when he knew it wouldn't make him all that popular before the king.

How about for us? It seems like a much easier path of living out the Gospel if it's just about my actions instead of my actions *and* my words. Sorry to disappoint, but actions alone simply don't cut it, and words alone don't cut it. As far as actions alone, Romans 10:14 makes this clear:

> How are they to call on one they have not believed in? And how are they to believe in one they have not heard of? And how are they to hear without someone preaching to them?

So what do the actions of the tentmaker do for the Gospel, then? How does work ethic matter if it's still all about the words spoken in evangelism?

Our actions in tentmaking do three things. They open the door for our witness; they give us the opportunity to evangelize; and they demonstrate how the Gospel works in the world. First, our actions open the door by our excellent quality of work. All of what was written in the previous chapters about the value and dignity of work still holds true. Our work allows us to use the best of our gifts to show people the integrity and change that Jesus has brought about in our lives. To put it in a scriptural context, take a look at Matthew 5.16:

> In the same way, let your light shine before people,
> so that they can see your good deeds and give hon-
> or to your Father in heaven.

They do see the good deeds, and the deeds give an introduction to our words.

Second, our work gives us the opportunity to be in
contact with the unreached. It allows us to meet them on
their home turf, so to speak, and share the most important relationship with them. They can process through
this in the context of their own home and friends and
family without the requirement of pulling them out of
their context to share the Good News with them.

Third, our actions model the order God intends for
the world. This, too, gives credence to the message we
bear by demonstrating a God-ordained approach to
work. Without this, we easily venture into dangerous
territory where we think that only our words matter. The
caricature, "Do as I say, not as I do," dangerously defines
missions as simply telling a message irrespective of the
morality or ethics that show all of God's intentions in his
mission for God's people.

Christopher Wright explains many of these actions for
the people of God in his book *The Mission of God's People*.
As a first step, he makes the distinction between *mission*
and *missions*. God has given his people a broad mission
that includes many actions such as ruling over all the
animals and all the earth, being fruitful and multiplying
over the face of the earth (Genesis 1.28), subduing the
earth, caring for the earth and maintaining it (Genesis
2.15), demonstrating justice and righteousness (Genesis 18.19), redemptively blessing the oppressed (Micah
6.8) and "representing God by living lives of practical
holiness in the midst of the world."[19] The final point that

Wright makes is that the Church is to send people with the express purpose of telling the Good News of Jesus' death and resurrection. This is missions.

So, the act of sending people with the message about Jesus is *missions* and is part of God's overarching *mission* for his people along with all of those other actions defined in the Bible. This is important in this context because all of those other actions of God's mission for his people establish the context of life change so that the message of the Gospel has meaning. Showing justice and righteousness in the face of the world's depravity is evidence that the Gospel has renewed your mind and it is at work in your life. Your care for the poor and oppressed shows that the things that break God's heart break your heart and that the Gospel is softening your emotions with the compassion of God. Your passionate work ethic in tentmaking is evidence that your mind is being renewed by the Gospel which is at work in your life.

These actions in your life do not supplant the need to share the message of the Gospel, but they do give credibility to the message you bear. A myopic definition of missions that does not include the actions of God's mission for his people runs the risk of hypocrisy.

Tentmaking certainly is not shying away from evangelism. Here is another New Testament example of this point. Timothy was a disciple of Paul, but more specifically he was a pastor. In fact, the two books written from Paul to Timothy along with Paul's book to Titus are called the Pastoral Epistles because of their thorough instruction on how to properly shepherd and care for a church. In spite of Timothy's "gifting" and "occupation" as a pastor, Paul gives him this direct command:

You, however, be self-controlled in all things, endure hardship, do an evangelist's work, fulfill your ministry.

2 Timothy 4.5

Timothy could have rightfully objected, "Wait a minute, Paul. I'm a pastor! My gifts are to be used in the Church with Christians. It's the evangelist's job to work with the Lost and Unreached, and it's my job to shepherd the people that the evangelist brings to the Lord." Apparently, Paul did not agree with this reductionism. Paul had the notion and gave the command that *no matter what your occupation, you should do the work of an evangelist.*

No matter what your occupation, you should do the work of an evangelist.

Tentmakers, especially, must be *excellent evangelists.* They must be excellent evangelists because they need to be able to seize the moments that lead to opportunities to share deeper truth in the midst of cross-cultural work. They need to constantly and boldly plant seeds in conversation that might grow into deeper understanding of the truth of Jesus. They need to do this with deftness of living out their work faithfully and living and speaking the truth, often in restrictive countries where they need to balance legal requirements about proselytization. This is not an easier way of witness, but it is the way of tentmakers.

Your actions matter because they are the foundation of your credibility just as Daniel's actions were the foundation of his credibility. Your words matter because there is no substitute for proclaiming the message of Jesus just as Daniel spoke his message boldly. The unreached are dying to hear the message you bear.

Principle 21
Perfect Submission Does Not Need a Perfect Government

One last lesson from chapter 5 can be drawn from verse 19:

> Due to the greatness that [God] bestowed on [your father, Nebuchadnezzar], all peoples, nations, and language groups were trembling with fear before him. He killed whom he wished, he spared whom he wished, he exalted whom he wished, and he brought low whom he wished.

Daniel lived under terrifying tyranny. His obedience to the king and his submission under that king was not predicated on the righteousness of that king or the perfection of the government of the land. In fact, as we have seen through Daniel's example, he was able to actively and significantly participate in the government of that tyrannical regime while being a force for good. Daniel didn't refuse to submit to the authority of the government, and he didn't move to Canada because his candidate wasn't elected. In the same way, we can serve God wherever we are.

I attended the University of Northwestern in Saint Paul, Minnesota, for my undergraduate degrees, and I often heard students complain about the required daily chapel attendance. For me, this requirement was the very reason I was at Northwestern. Northwestern was serious about the spiritual vitality of its students.

In fact, one of the most important lessons I learned in my studies was from a chapel talk by Ted Engstrom, the late president of Youth For Christ and World Vision. Ted Engstrom's life priorities became my life priorities that day:

1. God. Put him above parents, bosses, or governments that might contradict him.

2. Family. Look after your family as your most important earthly relationships.

3. Work. Scripture teaches that the one who does not provide for family is worse than an unbeliever (1 Timothy 5.8), so work must be next.

4. Everything else. Church volunteer ministry, hobbies, personal development, sports, and so many other things are good but only in their place. If they distract from any of the other three priorities, they are out of place.

Daniel had these same priorities in place. The real question is, when are obedience and submission to tyrannical governments appropriate? Daniel did disobey his government as we will see in the next chapter, but up to this point, Daniel lived under and served this tyrannical regime because it wasn't requiring him, personally, to disobey God. This would have included paying taxes, obeying laws, and giving quality advice that strengthened the abilities of the tyrannical regime. On the other hand, when it came to personal moral objection, Daniel stayed strong and obeyed his first priority—God.

Following Daniel's example, until the point that a tyrannical government personally requires you to disobey God, you must obey the government and its laws. At whatever point that government requires you to disobey God, you must be willing to say, as Peter and the apostles did, "We must obey God rather than people" (Acts 5.29).

DANIEL 6

Principle 22
It Ain't Over 'til It's Over

EARLIER WE LOOKED AT the artificial definition of a work week and how it is specifically tied to our industrialized society and even the Industrial Age. There is nothing written in the human moral code that says that a workweek is forty hours. In similar manner, there is nothing written in the human moral code that says retirement age is 60, 62.5, 65, 66 or 70. Although he doesn't cite Daniel as a biblical example, John Piper makes this point strongly in his book *Rethinking Retirement*. Daniel, Abraham, Moses, the Apostle John, and numerous others are examples of those who faithfully served the Lord even past the years when others would have deemed them incapable. They certainly didn't let an artificial declaration of retirement age dictate to them when they should stop work and take up shuffleboard in Florida.

> So Darius the Mede took control of the kingdom when he was about sixty-two years old.
> *Daniel 5.31*

Darius the Mede is introduced to us at the end of chapter 5 as he took over the kingdom from Belshazzar. This transpired in 539 B.C., which is sixty-six years after

Daniel hopped on the scene in 605 B.C. That means that Daniel would have been at least seventy-nine years old when he started his second career serving the king as head of all of the satraps of Darius' kingdom.

> It seemed like a good idea to Darius to appoint over the kingdom 120 satraps who would be in charge of the entire kingdom. Over them would be three supervisors, one of whom was Daniel. These satraps were accountable to them, so that the king's interests might not incur damage. Now this Daniel was distinguishing himself above the other supervisors and the satraps, for he had an extraordinary spirit. In fact, the king intended to appoint him over the entire kingdom.
>
> *Daniel 6.1-3*

If you are reading this and you are approaching or gliding past the time when you are expected to hang up your cleats, take a good look at this example of Daniel and ask yourself why you are planning to retire or why you did retire? Is it because you think you could no longer handle the busy schedule of work? I doubt it. Most retirees I know share how they didn't know what busy was until they retired. Is it because you think you are no longer valuable? Don't believe it. Someone who has all of the years of education and training and certifications and experience and wisdom behind them doesn't have to stumble through terrible mistakes because those were done long ago. Don't believe those voices that say that you have nothing to offer.

Is it medical problems that are holding you back? I think we can reasonably assume that old people in the Bible dealt with problems that old people deal with today.

I'm not sure that is entirely fair, though, since people in their 70s or 80s today have far more medical help than anyone in Daniel's day could ever have dreamed of. The comparison is unfair to Daniel, not unfair to you.

Is it time that is holding you back? You just don't feel you have time to serve the Lord through your occupation? Who is better prepared with freedom and flexibility than those who don't have young children to raise or kids to put through college?

Is it grandkids? Today's travel capabilities are astounding, and they really leave very little excuse. Most tentmaking jobs as foreign hires include round-trip airfare for the family each year. On top of that, the financial advantages of tentmaking can readily support multiple trips each year. With the ability to get almost anywhere in the world within about twenty-four hours, travel time to family is too quick to be a reason to keep people from tentmaking.

So, what is holding you back? I earnestly believe that retirees are a huge reservoir of untapped potential for the Kingdom of God, and tentmaking could be just the thing to bring out that potential as it was for Daniel.

For Daniel, it is likely that he sat unappreciated and unemployed for about two decades during the reign of Belshazzar. In spite of this, he kept his mind and skills sharp. After a single night of a powerful move by the Lord, Daniel was ready to serve the new king, Darius, and he was at the top of his game. As long as Daniel could contribute, he did contribute.

To model this, I want to share the story of a dear mentor of mine. Dr. Kyle Wilson was the Campus Pastor at the University of Northwestern during my years of study there. He also had been the director of the Male Chorus where I got to know him more closely. As he approached and passed "retirement age," he passed on his duties as director but continued to lead short-term mission trips as campus pastor. As he entered his 70s he explained that some felt he should retire in those years, so he tapered down his involvement at Northwestern and started a mission agency. Yes, as he entered his "retirement," he founded the Poland Evangelical Mission and has kept his energies moving strongly forward as long as he is physically able to contribute.

"Doc" Wilson had a good example to follow in Daniel, who established himself as a force of wisdom to be reckoned with just as he did in his younger years, quickly rising up the ranks. Next step for this Israelite, Executive VP of Babylon.

Principle 23
Reach the Unreached Wherever You Are

So, as an octogenarian, Daniel went back to work; but he didn't just take up his old job with the same company. God had different plans, specifically, two more Unreached People Groups for Daniel to work with. Up to this point, Daniel had experience with three Babylonian kings: (1) Nabonidus who was technically king during the exile of Judah, (2) Nabonidus' son, Nebuchadnezzar, who was appointed king and served as king while his father went on a sixty-five year excursion to Arabia, and (3) Nabonidus' grandson, Belshazzar. Even though Daniel was eighty years old at this point, he was led by the Lord to work with two more Unreached People Groups before his career was over, sharing the one, true God with the Medes, who were a people from an arc-shaped territory to the north of modern-day Iraq and Iran, and the Persians, who are synonymous with modern-day Iran.

Even though Daniel didn't move to a new location, the Lord brought to him a new people group to work with. These Medes overthrew the Babylonian empire, but as the prophecy to Belshazzar shows, the Lord controls the moves of powerful kingdoms, even the Babylonians and the Medo-Persians.

In our day, I look in wonder at the move of 100,000 Somalis from arid, hot Africa to freezing, snowbound Minneapolis. What would draw the largest population of Somalis outside of east Africa to make their homes among the saturation of Scandinavian descendents in Minnesota?

Let me share the Apostle Paul's words with you as the cause for this modern Somali immigration and ancient takeover by the Medes and Persians:

> From one man he made every nation of the human race to inhabit the entire earth, determining their set times and the fixed limits of the places where they would live. . .
>
> *Acts 17.26*

God is the one who not only orchestrates which kingdoms are victorious and which kingdoms get exiled to foreign lands, but he also orchestrates the times and fixed limits (boundaries) of the places where people live. When we ask how Daniel could seamlessly move from service to one kingdom to service of the occupying enemy kingdom—God did it. When we ask how 100,000 Somalis would choose a city of almost opposite culture and climate 13,396 kilometers away—God did it. In the 2000s, God decided that these Somalis would inhabit the boundaries of Minneapolis, Minnesota.

Here's the kicker. He has a purpose in this,

> . . . *so that they would search for God* and perhaps grope around for him *and find him*, though he is not far from each one of us.
>
> *Acts 17.27 (emphasis added)*

That's right, God decided that all those Somalis would leave Africa and take up root in freezing cold Minnesota so they would seek him out and find him. It was the same purpose for the Medo-Persians. It's for the same purpose God moved the Jews from Israel to Babylon, so that they might seek God *and* so that they might be there when these other people sought God. In the midst of your going to the nations, don't neglect the times and places where God may be bringing the nations to you. Again, take every opportunity the Lord brings to you to share faithfully the truth that means so much to you.

Principle 24
Prepare For Legal Persecution

We've witnessed the major shift in the thinking of Nebuchadnezzar as he came to recognize that the Most High God is the God of gods and Lord of lords. We've witnessed how this same truth was made clear to Belshazzar through Daniel's testimony. Now we are about to witness how the Lord makes this clear to Darius.

Verse 4 records for us the familiar script with familiar opposition and a familiar conspiracy:

> Consequently the supervisors and satraps were trying to find some pretext against Daniel in connection with administrative matters. But they were

unable to find any such damaging evidence, because he was trustworthy and guilty of no negligence or corruption.

Daniel 6.4

It can't be ascertained whether these conspirators were the same as the previous wise men who carried out their plan against Hananiah, Mishael, and Azariah in chapter 3 or whether this is a new crop that had ripened with the same jealousy. If these were the same men, their pernicious vendetta against righteousness is striking. In that case, they must simply have seen a way to get a new king on their side. Obviously, the miraculous survival of the three men through a fiery furnace was not enough to bring them to the recognition that "heaven rules" (Daniel 4.26). This, then, is another opportunity to murder an innocent person who lives a righteous life, which is something that burns in the hearts of these men. Their hatred of righteous ones shows the truth of Jesus' simplification:

You have heard that it was said to an older generation, "Do not murder," and "whoever murders will be subjected to judgment." But I say to you that anyone who is angry with a brother will be subjected to judgment. And whoever insults a brother will be brought before the council, and whoever says "Fool" will be sent to fiery hell.

Matthew 5.21-22

These men went straight from burning jealousy to hatred to conspiring murder.

If this is a new group of conspirators, it is further evidence of the depravity of humankind that a mirror situation could repeat itself in the same locale with different people separated by only a few decades. Whether these are the same actors or a new batch, the wickedness in the heart of man is clearly demonstrated by their actions.

The means by which these men execute their collusion against Daniel are to attack his faithful obedience in following the Lord. They aren't going to ensnare him with the enticements that most people fall prey to, that is, "the desire of the flesh and the desire of the eyes and the arrogance produced by material possessions" to put it in the words of the Apostle John (1 John 2.16). Notwithstanding, they are undeterred. They contrive a plan to make illegal what Daniel does in his righteousness.

To this end, their Private Investigator comes back with good news that they can get him by making prayer illegal.

> For the next thirty days anyone who prays to any god or human other than you, O king, should be thrown into a den of lions.
>
> *Daniel 6.7*

We know this story so well that we easily skip over the fact that this was real life for Daniel. We skip to the Sunday School ending when Daniel survives a night with kitty cats, but Daniel had real emotions to contend with in his faithfulness. He was an old man, and he had no idea what his end would be. For all we know, he passed peacefully in his sleep years after the book of Daniel was concluded, but at this point, he did not know the outcome of this urgent situation.

His thoughts probably went something like this, "Well, they've finally done it. They've found a way to kill me after all of these years. I knew it was coming sometime. I've lived for sixty-five years with this threat always at my door. I know they've wanted to kill me, and I thought my life was protected by righteous living. 'God, why this way? Why now?' I guess now is as good a time as any. I will now choose to meet my end." In his mind, it was as much a death sentence as the guillotine or the electric chair or the firing squad or the hangman's noose or the needle. He had no promise from God that he would not die this way and it seemed by all accounts that his detractors had won.

Nonetheless, Daniel remains faithful. He goes to pray.

Making prayer illegal was a tactic that "ensnared" the righteous in Daniel's time, but it seems that there are many possible entrapments that could be used against those proclaiming righteousness in our time. For example, the Bible categorizes homosexuality as immoral. Soon, that categorization will be considered a hate crime, and Christians will be arrested for affirming passages like 1 Corinthians 6.9-10:

> Do you not know that the unrighteous will not inherit the kingdom of God? Do not be deceived! The sexually immoral, idolaters, adulterers, passive homosexual partners, practicing homosexuals, thieves, the greedy, drunkards, the verbally abusive, and swindlers will not inherit the kingdom of God.

Public affirmations of biblical truths such as monuments of the Ten Commandments will be seen as an affront to the conscience of atheists. Teaching children biblical Creationism will be classified as corruption of young minds. Refusing to service immoral sexual unions at hotels, bakeries, wedding facilities, catering companies, and churches will result in the removal of any tax exempt benefits. Subsequent lawsuits will force morally grounded groups out of business.

As far as the comparison to Daniel's delivery from the lion's den, again, there is no promise from God that followers of Jesus will not endure this sort of persecution. To the contrary, Jesus himself says, "And you will be hated by everyone because of my name" (Matthew 10.22), and Paul says, "Now in fact all who want to live godly lives in Christ Jesus will be persecuted" (2 Timothy 3.12). Of course, these words are not spoken to make us pessimistic or alarmed about what is to come, but rather, they are spoken so that we will not be surprised when it does happen, and we will know that even through this, God is in control. These words are spoken to strengthen us in the face of that persecution to have a similar resolve to Daniel when he faced certain death by lions. To borrow the words of Daniel's friends from chapter 3,

If our God whom we are serving exists, he is able to rescue us from the furnace of blazing fire, and he will rescue us, O king, from your power as well. But if not, let it be known to you, O king, that we don't serve your gods, and we will not pay homage to the golden statue that you have erected.

Daniel 3.17

Let me map this text out in a different way for you to see the exercise of your faith:

IF God exists,

THEN he can rescue

AND **we will not worship
the statue**

ELSE IF God does not exist,

THEN **we will not worship the statue**

OR IF God does not save,

THEN **we will not worship the statue**

CONCLUSION: **We will not worship
the statue.**

With a similar formula, we can fill in whatever threat we are facing,

IF God exists,

THEN he can [[SAVING ACTION]]

AND **we remain faithful**

ELSE IF God does not exist,

THEN **we remain faithful**

OR IF God does not [[SAVING ACTION]],

THEN **we remain faithful**

CONCLUSION: **We remain faithful.**

However, there are a few edits needed for this formula that Daniel's friends and Daniel himself would have made. First, God's existence was not in question in any way. Second, God's ability was not in question, especially after the first miracle. So, the formula becomes,

God does [[SAVING ACTION]]

THEN **we remain faithful**

ELSE God does not [[SAVING ACTION]]

THEN we remain faithful

CONCLUSION: **We remain faithful.**

No matter what the persecution or trial or travail is that you encounter, God can overcome it. Sometimes he chooses to remove the trial and sometimes he chooses to provide grace through the trial, but our response should always be the same. Remain faithful.

Principle 25
Live an Authentic Life

When Daniel realized that a written decree had been issued, he entered his home, where the windows in his upper room opened toward Jerusalem. Three times daily he was kneeling and offering prayers and thanks to his God just as he had been accustomed to do previously.

Daniel 6.10

I've often asked myself what I would do if I received a diagnosis of a terminal illness, or worse, if I suddenly knew I had only a few days to live. If I had three-to-six months to live, would I get on a plane and live out my last days boldly proclaiming the Lord among the unreached? Would I, instead, spend those days frantically writing out years of thoughts and experiences so that I could leave a legacy in books and articles? Would I abandon normal work and simply spend that time, even if it was an indefinite length, quietly living with my family and friends who are closest to me? Would a vacation or cruise be an appropriate way to enjoy all that this life has to offer?

All things considered, I shouldn't do much other than what I am already doing. If I am obediently following the Lord, I am already doing what God has called and gifted me to do, and I should continue to do that as long as I have breath. Even with such a difficult diagnosis, there should be no panic or fear since I know I am doing what the Lord wants me to do, and I know where I am going when the Lord wants me to go.

Of course, these words are more easily said than lived out, and if that day ever comes that I receive such a diagnosis, I hope that I will respond with this faith. Even so, Daniel records for us that he did just that when he received what, by all accounts, would have been considered a death sentence. He knew he was trapped by the unchangeable law of the Medes and Persians, and he had every reason to believe that the end had come. What did he do?

Daniel did what he was accustomed to doing. He did what he normally did. He took his siesta for prayer at his home, and he offered thanks and prayed to the Lord just like always. What I would hope would be my highest achievement of calm, reasoned faith is what Daniel actually did when the time came.

The principle for us to glean from this, then, is that our lives should be authentic through and through. There should be no duplicity of leading a double life. There should be no sacred/secular divide in what we do. There should be no compartmentalization of what we do on Sundays before the Lord and what we do the rest of the week by ourselves. That is an authentic life.

SECTION 3

DOES IT WORK?

AFTER ALL OF THIS DISCUSSION, does tent-making really work among the unreached? Do people really come to worship and serve the Most High God because of the faithful work and words of tentmakers? How can it make that much of a difference just by continuing work that you would be doing anyway in your home country? To answer this, let's look back at Daniel's story.

> How great are his signs!
> How mighty are his wonders!
> His kingdom will last forever,
> and his authority continues from one
> generation to the next.
>
> *Daniel 4.3*

> I extolled the Most High,
> and I praised and glorified the one who
> lives forever.
> For his authority is an everlasting authority,
> and his kingdom extends from one generation to
> the next.
> All the inhabitants of the earth are regarded
> as nothing.

> He does as he wishes with the army of heaven
>   and with those who inhabit the earth.
> No one slaps his hand
>   and says to him, "What have you done?"
>   *Daniel 4.34-35*

> For he is the living God;
> he endures forever.
> His kingdom will not be destroyed;
> his authority is forever.
> He rescues and delivers
> and performs signs and wonders
> in the heavens and on the earth.
>   *Daniel 6.26-27*

Those are amazing declarations of praise to God that sound as though they could have just as easily been plucked from the Psalms rather than the book of Daniel. They are indicative of people who have personal knowledge of God and experience personal worship of God.

But these aren't the words of Daniel or some other Jewish hero of the faith. They aren't even the words of some faithful but obscure Jewish follower like the farmer Amos. Rather, these are the words of two kings, one Babylonian and one Medo-Persian. These words spoken by Nebuchadnezzar and Darius were not spoken during some weak point in their kingdoms when they were begging for help from any god who would listen. These proclamations of praise were spoken by the most powerful men of the most powerful kingdoms at the pinnacle of their careers. Even in the midst of all of that power, they recognized their position beneath the Creator of all of the universe.

St. Francis of Assisi had a wild idea. This wild idea started when he was a soldier and he began to see the horrible acts of violence that humans are capable of executing against one another. These acts of violence drove him to a monastic life where he disavowed all possessions and became an absolute pacifist. During the Crusades through which he lived, a pacifist's life was not one that was highly regarded. Nonetheless, he had a wild idea to end the inconceivable brutality he witnessed from both the Christians and the Muslims. His wild idea was to walk across enemy lines to be captured by the same Muslim soldiers who dismembered and disfigured Christian prisoners of war. In his capture, the soldiers would see that he had no worldly possessions save the coarse, brown robe he wore as clothing. He carried no weapon since he was not a soldier. He carried no message since he was not a spy. He would allow himself to be captured and ask to speak to the sultan himself. His aim was to bring peace between the world's two greatest religions and end a series of heinous, brutal wars.

St. Francis did get an audience with the sultan, or ruler, of the Muslims, Saladin. In fact, St. Francis and Saladin established a strong friendship as Saladin gave extraordinary hospitality to his Christian guest. In the end, St. Francis came very close to achieving his wild idea but not close enough.[20]

Compare those valiant efforts with the unassuming presence of a faithful, young Jewish man named Daniel who simply did his work to the best of his ability while taking every opportunity to stand for righteousness in the midst of a foreign kingdom that was not honoring righteousness. Despite his intentionality, St. Francis did not succeed, whereas Daniel did. Through Daniel's powerful integration of faith and work and his faithfulness through decades of slave labor, he led two enemy kings to faith in his God. As far as the other two kings he served faithfully under, Belshazzar certainly recognized the superiority and power of the Most High God although his life was cut short by the end of his kingdom. We can only speculate about the influence Daniel had in Cyrus' life, with the exception that "this Daniel prospered during the reign of Darius and the reign of Cyrus the Persian."

We know from history that Cyrus became one of the most admired kings of ancient Persia that Persian people still hold in high regard today. Within one year of coming to rule over the Medo-Persian Empire and its control of Babylonia, King Cyrus issued his famous decree that allowed the Jewish captives to return to their homeland of Israel.

In the first year of King Cyrus of Persia, in order to fulfill the Lord's message spoken through Jeremiah, the Lord stirred the mind of King Cyrus of Persia. He disseminated a proclamation throughout his entire kingdom, announcing in a written edict the following:

"Thus says King Cyrus of Persia:

"'The Lord God of heaven has given me all the kingdoms of the earth. He has instructed me to build a temple for him in Jerusalem, which is in Judah. Anyone from his people among you (may his God be with him!) may go up to Jerusalem, which is in Judah, and may build the temple of the Lord God of Israel—he is the God who is in Jerusalem. Anyone who survives in any of those places where he is a resident foreigner must be helped by his neighbors with silver, gold, equipment, and animals, along with voluntary offerings for the temple of God which is in Jerusalem.'"

Ezra 1.1-4

How much influence did Daniel have on this policy? We cannot know for certain, but at the very least, we can say that Daniel led two kings from two Unreached People Groups to faith in the Most High God, he led another king to clear recognition of the rule and authority of the Most High God, and he faithfully prospered and served under another king who made a unilateral decision to allow Daniel's captive people to return to their homeland.

Tentmaking has impact.

FINAL THOUGHTS

Creating an Environment of Intrigue

IN 1974, BILLY GRAHAM organized the First International Congress on World Evangelization. Out of that conference, the Lausanne Covenant was drawn up, named after the city where the congress was held. As early as that first meeting in 1974, one of the components of the Lausanne Covenant was a fifty-nine-page document titled Marketplace Ministry. The ideas about work described in *Work of Influence* are not new. Rather, they are a renewed call to what followers of God have been doing since the time of the patriarchs, including the days of Daniel.

Billy Graham said, "I believe that one of the next great moves of God is going to be through the believers in the workplace."[21] The aim of this book is to mobilize and equip such a massive movement of believers in the workplace. To that end, we have defined key terms to forge the path forward and encourage people to take heed of the billions of people who have not heard the Good News of Jesus. These people do not know even a single follower of Jesus. They do not have Bibles to read; they do not have sermon podcasts to listen to or radio programs in their languages. They do not have churches to go to or TV programs to give them even an opportunity to weigh the claims of the Bible. This is the situation for the unreached, and our commission is to give them the opportunity to choose Jesus for themselves.

These faithful witnesses can effectively share the Gospel by actively creating an environment of intrigue while doing their best work to the glory of God.

For many of these people, the only way of giving them this opportunity is for someone to go to them personally. In the process of living and working among them, these faithful witnesses can effectively share the Gospel by actively creating an environment of intrigue while doing their best work to the glory of God. Through astute preparation and planning and a massive movement of prayer, interested individuals can follow the pattern of twenty-five principles we can observe from the lives of Daniel, Hananiah, Azariah, and Mishael. These principles not only highlight finding joy in doing our best work and making our best contribution to the world, but they highlight vast insight from building deep personal relationships to language acquisition to living in humility to knowing the limits of syncretism. Through authentic lives impact is made. As in the example of Daniel who served before four kings and saw two of them make professions of faith in the Most High God, faithful witnesses will see results through perseverance and active engagement with the unreached. Tentmaking is the next great move of God. It actively puts forward a plan for you to get the most joy by doing your best work and serving the Lord as he commissioned you to do.

Get the most joy by doing your best work and serving the Lord as he commissioned you to do.

What Next?

Of course, many steps have been laid out in the preceding pages for you to actively study and prepare to work among the unreached, but what practical steps can you take to learn more and prepare more? Here are four areas you can use to prepare yourself: Go, Live, Pray, Give.

Go.

So you've caught the vision, and you want to go. You want to be used by the Lord to live and work among the unreached. It's a powerful conclusion to come to, and it's a thrilling place to be in your life. One of the major questions you will need to answer is whether you go independently or with an organization, and there are advantages and disadvantages with each.

One of the major advantages of going with an organization is an umbrella advantage that affects many different elements of living and working overseas. The advantage is that when you go with an organization, you are not recreating the wheel. They've been there, done that. It's the organization's business to know what sort of training people need or what counseling requirements they might need so that issues from the past don't come up overseas that cause a premature departure. Organizations know how to help you relate to your home church and how to take care of your children. Organizations are good at lining you up with other like-minded people for support and strength overseas. They are also a great source of support through conferences or gatherings that keep the fire alive during years of living far away from your home country.

That being said, some people prefer not being attached to an organization so that they can say with a clear conscience to anyone who asks that they are not part of a sending agency. This is an important consideration. Some people also prefer the natural relationships with like-minded people that they build overseas rather than "artificial" relationships that are formed because people might be part of the same organization. Going without an organization can also be a fast track to getting overseas. Rather than having to jump through organizational requirements, tentmakers can simply acquire a contract and go. So tentmaking can be done with or without an organization whether receiving financial support from the organization or not.

Irrespective of whether you go with an organization, consider further training. These points of tentmaking have been addressed in a cursory fashion to lay the groundwork for much more study and preparation. One good place to go deeper is a formal training program like the courses on tentmaking from Professionals Global (www.professionalsglobal.org) or language acquisition courses, Church Planting Movement (Disciple Making Movement) courses, or security courses.

Live.

What life are you living now? Are you living a life that generously and liberally shares the Gospel? When I went overseas longterm, I first went with an organization, Arab World Ministries (AWM). As part of the interview process, I was asked by AWM to sketch my neighborhood or apartment building in the United States and write in as many of my neighbors' names as I could. What was the point of this? After all, it was unlikely that I lived in an exclusively Arab neighborhood, so my neighbors weren't necessarily relevant to my ministry with AWM. Or were they?

The point of the exercise was this: if you don't do it here, you won't do it there. If you're not sharing your faith here, you can't expect suddenly to become a person who will share your faith there. Jesus didn't give us the option of picking and choosing whom to share with. So, AWM's request of this simple sketch was a clever vetting tool used to identify who is connecting with their neighbors enough to learn their names.

That being the case, what sort of person will you be? You are aiming to be a source of light in the lives of the unreached. Is the light shining brightly in your own life? Are you cultivating the habits and disciplines now that will sustain you then? Are you dealing with conflict and problems and issues in an intentional, forgiving way now, or are you sweeping them under the rug with the hope that after a few years of living overseas they will disappear?

Several years ago I came across a great little book by Dennis Okholm titled *Monk Habits for Everyday People: Benedictine Spirituality for Protestants*.[22] The book's action steps here are practical and meaningful:

1. Pray at least two offices (written prayers) daily.

2. Read and meditate on Scripture.

3. Practice silence.

4. Practice contemplative prayer.

5. Recognize that every moment is lived before God.

6. Fast each week.

7. Attend church.

8. Care for those in your community.

9. Treat your family and work as your main ministry.

10. Instead of judging, pray.

11. Be involved in a church program.

12. Treat possessions with care and reverence.

13. Be stable.

14. Serve others.

These are not a collection of works to gain favor before God but, rather, disciplines that will draw you closer to the Savior and build rapport with those around you.

Pray.

Begin to build your massive movement of prayer now. Share with others, particularly your church, your thoughts and how the Lord is moving on your heart. Enlist trusted advisors now who can speak into your life and guide you as you take these steps forward. Pray with your family for the people you hope to work with.

One resource I recommend for this is Prayercast.com where you will find attractive video shorts with national speakers praying for every country around the globe. These can be used for you and others to quickly learn about your host country and those countries in the region you will be living.

Think creatively about how you can incorporate friends and family into a trusted network of people that will stand with you through thick and thin. One of those people for me has been Chuck Oehmcke, my best friend's father. I grew up in a single-parent home. In the absence of my father, Chuck became a father to me in many ways. Through each major transition in my life since my teenage years, he has been there providing consistent, wise counsel, encouragement, and faithful prayer. This enduring input of prayer in my life has left an indelible impact that has shaped who I am today.

Give.

If there's one thing that will direct your heart, it's this: your money. If you see the need to mobilize tentmakers and get them actively involved, you are showing that you treasure and value sharing the Good News through tentmaking. Take a look at Jesus' words about money and treasure:

> Do not accumulate for yourselves treasures on earth, where moth and rust destroy and where thieves break in and steal. But accumulate for yourselves treasures in heaven, where moth and rust do not destroy, and thieves do not break in and steal. For where your treasure is, there your heart will be also.
>
> The eye is the lamp of the body. If then your eye is healthy, your whole body will be full of light. But if your eye is diseased, your whole body will be full of darkness. If then the light in you is darkness, how great is the darkness!
>
> No one can serve two masters, for either he will hate the one and love the other, or he will be devoted to the one and despise the other. You cannot serve God and money.
>
> *Matthew 6.19-24*

Why are the words about the eye and the lamp of the body included above? The reason is that they are tied to the context by the bookends about money. If your eye sees things as they really are, it shows you are healthy. On the other hand, if you see things as they are but don't align your life to how things really are, your bodily actions don't match what your eyes see.

This passage is stating that if you recognize the importance of eternal things such as the need for the Gospel in people's lives (your eye sees the reality of the situation) but you prioritize earthly treasures above eternal treasures (a diseased view of reality), how great is the darkness! Instead, align your actions with the real needs you see because you cannot serve God and money.

So, give! If you see the need, be a part of the solution. There are many organizations you can give to in order to see the Good News go forward. Be a part of the solution now, and in so doing, show that the values and priorities that hold your heart are given to you by Jesus.

May God graciously guide your steps as you go for his glory and your joy.

εἰς τὴν δόξαν τοῦ θεοῦ

dave@4God.pro

APPENDIX

Summary of the Principles

Principle 1
Tentmaking Is a Spiritual Battle

Recognize that the enemy will be hard against you using whatever tactics he can to unseat you. Tentmaking is living on the front lines of this battle.

Principle 2
God Is in Control

Even through difficult times when it seems the enemy is winning, God is still in control and he will guide your steps.

Principle 3
Go to the Places of Greatest Need

The Lost and the Unreached have the same spiritual need to know Jesus, but the Unreached are restricted from hearing the Good News. Be part of finishing the Great Commission by going to the Unreached.

Principle 4
Do Not Think More Highly of Yourself than You Ought, or "Humility and How I Attained It"

Let humility be your guiding principle even when the world might see that you have something to boast about.

Principle 5
You Cannot Serve God and Yen

Tentmaking has the potential of being lucrative. Take care that your income is not your motivation. What will you do with the "king's delicacies" entrusted to you?

Principle 6
Your Work Has Intrinsic Value

Take the mindset of a craftsman understanding that you make a unique contribution through the work you do. Your work is not just a means to an end, but it has intrinsic value.

Principle 7
Read Everything

Become an expert in the people you serve. Read everything available in order to glean all of the cultural clues available for witness.

Principle 8
Major on the Majors

Use discernment to think through in advance where your moral boundaries will be. Be sure that you place those boundaries on things that matter to prevent unnecessary offense.

Principle 9
Be Audacious

Build and use relational capital to your advantage without exploiting people or crossing the line of corruption.

Principle 10
Understand God's Ways with People

Recognize that God works in different ways with different people groups. What is persuasive to you may have no impact on others. On the other hand, whole people groups may be moved to faith by something that is not motivating for you.

Principle 11
Be Winsome to Win Some

Make yourself into someone pleasant that people want to be around. Smooth the rough edges in your own personality so that people will listen to your greatest message.

Principle 12
Initiate a Massive Movement of Prayer

Recognize the incredible power of prayer, and be sure you have an army of people judiciously praying with you in your tentmaking experience.

Principle 13
Respond in Faith

When God makes the way clear, step out in faith. Cultivate such a close relationship to the Lord that you recognize his direction immediately and act on it without hesitation.

Principle 14
You Can't Clean a Fish before You Catch It

Know that you can't expect people to act in a moral manner when they are blind to the truth of Jesus. Without the Lord renewing their lives, they can't be expected to live moral lives of believers.

Principle 15
You Will Encounter Slanderous Opposition

One of the enemy's most powerful tools is gossip and slander. Without a doubt, you will encounter these, but guard your own heart by always responding in a biblical, honorable manner.

Principle 16
Beware of Syncretism

As people see truth in your words, their natural inclination will simply be to append that truth to their worldview. Patiently work with them to correct this syncretism as they walk toward the Lord's regeneration of their minds.

Principle 17
Sanctification Is a Process

Even after people make a profession of faith, they still need to learn how to live as followers of Jesus and remove sin wherever it can be identified in their lives. Be understanding as you walk with them through this process, knowing that they can only change what they recognize as wrong.

Principle 18
The Most High God Is King of Kings and Lord of Lords

Given the nature of who God is, recognize that he is sovereign over the hearts of kings and even over our biggest problems. He controls it all and he can move in amazing ways in the hearts of people.

Principle 19
In the World but Not of the World

In your work, you will see and hear much that is distasteful to you as a believer. Nonetheless, your calling is to be in that milieu in order to walk people out of it through faith.

Principle 20
Preach the Gospel at All Times

Your actions through your work ethic speak of who you are as a follower of Jesus. Be courageous in speaking the words necessary to explain why you have this hope within you.

Principle 21
Perfect Submission Does Not Need a Perfect Government

Our obedience to governing authorities is not contingent on those authorities acting in a godly manner. We are called to obey those authorities at all times up to the point that obedience contradicts our moral responsibility to God.

Principle 22
It Ain't Over 'til It's Over

"Retirement age" doesn't mean hanging up your cleats and heading to the beach. Use your years of experience, skills, relationships, and stature to serve the Lord as a tentmaker during some of the richest years of your life.

Principle 23
Reach the Unreached Wherever You Are

The Lord has determined the times and dwelling places of even the unreached. Be open to the Lord's influence through your work wherever you are, not just "over there."

Principle 24
Prepare For Legal Persecution

Jesus informed us beforehand that the world will hate us because of him. We will have opposition. Hold strong even through those difficult times as further evidence of your faith and trust in him.

Principle 25
Live an Authentic Life

Be the same person of integrity no matter where you are or whom you are with. Even if you would be living out your last days of a terminal illness, be the same person without giving in to a sacred/secular divide of your life.

NOTES

1. Keller, 35.

2. https://www.ethnologue.com/statistics

3. https://www.ethnologue.com/enterprise-faq/how-many-languages-world-are-unwritten-0

4. Map generated as a personal favor by Loren Muehlius, LightSys, www.lightsys.org.

5. Statistics courtesy of Joshua Project https://joshuaproject.net/

6. Scott, Kindle edition.

7. Hale, Kindle edition.

8. Blaiklock 150.

9. Newport 28.

10. Wrzesniewski's study is cited in Newport 15.

11. Newport 19.

12. Citations from Brother Lawrence's book are taken from digital editions found at https://www.gutenberg.org/ebooks/5657.

13. Dave Sable shared this excellent speech at a *DonorDirect.com Conference* in Dallas in May of 2017. He shared his speaker's notes for the purpose of inclusion in this book.

14. This personal communication was part of Dr. Muska's lectures in his *Old Testament Survey* course.

15. Richardson, *Eternity in Their Hearts*.

16. Eadicicco, Lisa. "The Cofounder of Apple Talks about What It Was like to Work with Steve Jobs

When the Company Was Failing." *Business Insider*, 14 September 2015, www.businessinsider.com/apple-steve-wozniak-steve-jobs-2015-9.

17. https://lumina.bible.org/bible/Daniel+3

18. TED talks are inspirational video recordings on various topics by talented individuals. https://www.ted.com/talks

19. Wright 128.

20. Moses, *The Saint and the Sultan*, especially chapter 13.

21. Whitaker, www.twotenmag.com/magazine/issue-5/features/billy-graham-messenger-of-hope/

22. The action steps here are my summary of Okholm's steps.

BIBLIOGRAPHY

Baldwin, Joyce G. *Daniel.* Inter-varsity Press, 1978.

Barker, Kenneth, and John R. Kohlenberger. *Zondervan NIV Bible Commentary: Volume 2: New Testament.* Zondervan, 1994.

Barker, Ken. *Zondervan NASB Study Bible: Black Bonded Leather.* Zondervan, 2000.

Blaiklock, E.M. *The Acts of the Apostles.* Eerdmans, 1979.

Carson, D.A., Douglas J. Moo, Leon Morris. *An Introduction To the New Testament.* Zondervan, 1992.

Hale, Thomas. *Authentic Lives: Overcoming the Problem of Hidden Identity in Outreach to Restrictive Nations.* William Carey Library, 2016.

Harreld, Donald. "An Economic History of the World since 1400." *Audible.com,* 2016, www.audible.com/pd/History/An-Economic-History-of-the-World-since-1400-Audiobook/B01K4ZNTFS.

Joshua Project. https://joshuaproject.net/ accessed 2017.11.18

Keller, Timothy. *Every Good Endeavor.* Riverhead Books, 2012.

Lawrence, Brother. *The Practice of the Presence of God.* Project Gutenberg, 1 May 2004, www.gutenberg.org/ebooks/5657.

Losch, Dale. *A Better Way: Make Disciples Wherever Life Happens.* Crossworld, 2012.

Moses, Paul. *The Saint and the Sultan: the Crusades, Islam, and Francis of Assisi's Mission of Peace*. Doubleday Religion, 2009.

Newport, Cal. *So Good They Can't Ignore You: Why Skills Trump Passion in the Quest For Work You Love*. Hatchett Book Group, 2012.

Okholm, Dennis L. *Monk Habits for Everyday People: Benedictine Spirituality for Protestants*. Brazos Press, 2008.

Pfeiffer, Charles F., et al. *The Wycliffe Bible Encyclopedia: Volume 1, A-J*. Moody Press, 1975.

Pfeiffer, Charles F., et al. *The Wycliffe Bible Encyclopedia: Volume 2, K-Z*. Moody Press, 1975.

Phillips, Richard D. *The Masculine Mandate: God's Calling to Men*. Reformation Trust Publishing, 2016.

Piper, John, and Justin Taylor. *Rethinking Retirement: Finishing Life for the Glory of Christ*. Crossway Books, 2009.

Richardson, Don. *Eternity in Their Hearts*. Bethany House, 2014.

Sable, Dave. Personal communication.

Scott, Andrew. *Scatter: Go Therefore and Take Your Job with You*. Moody Publishers, 2016.

Simons, Gary F. and Charles D. Fennig (eds.). 2018. *Ethnologue: Languages of the World, Twenty-first edition*. Dallas, Texas: SIL International. Online version: http://www.ethnologue.com.

The NET Bible: a New Approach to Translation, Thoroughly Documented with 60,932 Notes. Biblical Studies Press, 2005.

Whitaker, Mark. "Billy Graham: Messenger Of Hope." *Two Ten Magazine*, 2013, www.twotenmag.com/magazine/issue-5/features/billy-graham-messenger-of-hope/. accessed 2017.12.14.

Wright, Christopher J.H. *The Mission of God's People: A Biblical Theology of the Church's Mission*. Grand Rapids, Michigan, Zondervan. 2010.

Wrzesniewski, Amy, et al. "Jobs, Careers, and Callings: People's Relations to Their Work." *Journal of Research in Personality*, vol. 31, no. 1, 1997, pp. 21–33.